THE COLLECTED WORKS OF
HENRIK IBSEN

VOLUME IV

PEER GYNT

(1867)

THE COLLECTED WORKS OF
HENRIK IBSEN
COPYRIGHT EDITION

VOLUME IV
PEER GYNT
A DRAMATIC POEM

TRANSLATED BY
WILLIAM AND CHARLES ARCHER

WITH INTRODUCTION BY
WILLIAM ARCHER

NEW YORK
CHARLES SCRIBNER'S SONS
1909

CONTENTS

PEER GYNT.

INTRODUCTION.*

THE publication of *Brand*, in March 1866, brought Ibsen fame (in Scandinavia) and relieved him from the immediate pressure of poverty. Two months later the Storthing voted him a yearly "poet-pension" of £90; and with this sum, as he wrote to the Minister who had been mainly instrumental in furthering his claim, he felt "his future assured," so that he could henceforth "devote himself without hindrance to his calling." This first glimpse of worldly prosperity, no doubt, brought with it the lighter mood which distinguishes *Peer Gynt* from its predecessor. To call it the gayest of Ibsen's works is not, perhaps, to say very much. Its satire, indeed, is bitter enough; but it is not the work of an unhappy man. The character of Peer Gynt, and many of his adventures, are conceived with unmistakable gusto. Some passages even bear witness to an exuberance of animal spirits which reminds one of Ben Jonson's saying with regard to Shakespeare—"aliquando sufflaminandus erat."

The summer of 1866 Ibsen spent at Frascati, in the Palazzo Gratiosi, where he lived "most

comfortably and cheaply." He found Frascati
and Tusculum "indescribably delightful." From
the windows of his study he could see Soracte,
" rising isolated and beautiful from the level of
the immense plain . . . the battlefield where the
chief engagement in the world's history took
place." So he writes in a letter to Paul Botten-
Hansen, and immediately afterwards proceeds:
" I shall soon be setting to work in good earnest.
I am still wrestling with my subject, but I know
that I shall get the upper hand of the brute before
long, and then everything will go smoothly."
But was the play here referred to *Peer Gynt?*
Perhaps not. From a letter to his publisher,
Hegel, written three months later, we learn that
at that time he was still turning over several
themes in his mind, and that one of them dealt
with the period of Christian IV. of Denmark. It
is in a letter to Hegel, dated from Rome, Janu-
ary 5, 1867, that we find the first unmistakable
reference to *Peer Gynt:* " Now I must tell you
that my new work is well under way, and will,
if nothing untoward happens, be finished early in
the summer. It is to be a long dramatic poem,
having as its chief figure one of the Norwegian
peasantry's half-mythical, fantastic heroes of *re-
cent* times. It will bear no resemblance to *Brand,*
contain no direct polemics and so forth. I have
long had the subject in my thoughts; now the
entire plan is worked out and written down, and
the first act begun. The thing grows as I work
at it, and I am certain that you will be satisfied
with it."

Two months later (March 8) the poem has " ad-
vanced to the middle of the second act." On

August 8, he sends to Hegel, from Villa Pisani,
Casamicciola, Ischia, the complete manuscript of
the first three acts, and writes: " I am curious to
hear how you like the poem. I am very hopeful
myself. It may interest you to know that Peer
Gynt is a real person, who lived in Gudbrandsdal,
probably at the end of last, or beginning of this,
century; but of his exploits not much more is
known than is to be found in Asbjörnsen's *Norwegian Fairy Tales*, in the section *Pictures from
the Mountains*. Thus I have not had very much
to build upon; but so much the more liberty has
been left me. It would interest me to know what
Clemens Petersen thinks of the work." What
Clemens Petersen did think we shall presently
learn.

On October 18 Ibsen despatched from Sorrento
the remainder of his manuscript, and the book
was published on November 14. It has often been
pointed out (by myself among others) as a very
remarkable fact that two such gigantic creations
as *Brand* and *Peer Gynt* should have been given
to the world in two successive years; but on ex-
amination the marvel somewhat dwindles. *Peer
Gynt* did not follow so hot-foot upon *Brand* as
the bare dates of publication would lead us to
suppose. *Brand* was written in the summer of
1865, *Peer Gynt* (as we have seen) in 1867; so
that the poet's mind had lain fallow for a whole
year (1866) between the two great efforts. It was
a long delay in the publication of *Brand* that
made its successor seem to tread so close upon its
heels.

One or two other references to the origin of
Peer Gynt may be found in Ibsen's letters. The

most important occurs in an autobiographical communication to Peter Hansen, dated Dresden, October 28, 1870: " After *Brand* came *Peer Gynt*, as though of itself. It was written in Southern Italy, in Ischia and at Sorrento. So far away from one's readers one becomes reckless. This poem contains much that has its origin in the circumstances of my own youth. My own mother —with the necessary exaggerations—served as the model for Åse. (Likewise for Inga in *The Pretenders*)." Twelve years later (1882) Ibsen wrote to George Brandes: " My father was a merchant with a large business and wide connections, and he enjoyed dispensing reckless hospitality. In 1836 he failed, and nothing was left to us except a farm near the town. . . . In writing *Peer Gynt*, I had the circumstances and memories of my own childhood before me when I described the life in the house of ' the rich Jon Gynt.' "

Returning to the above-quoted letter to Peter Hansen, we find this further allusion to *Peer Gynt* and its immediate predecessor and successor in the list of Ibsen's works: " Environment has great influence upon the forms in which imagination creates. May I not, like Christoff in *Jakob von Tyboe*,[1] point to *Brand* and *Peer Gynt*, and say: ' See, the wine-cup has done this?' And is there not something in *The League of Youth* [written in Dresden] that suggests ' Knackwurst und Bier'? Not that I would thereby imply any inferiority in the latter play." The transition to prose was no doubt an inevitable step in the evolution of Ibsen's genius; but one wishes he had kept to the " wine-cup " a little longer.

[1] One of Holberg's most famous comedies.

A masterpiece is not a flawless work, but one which has sufficient vitality to live down its faults, until at last we no longer heed, and almost forget, them. *Peer Gynt* had real faults, not a few; and its great merit, as some of us think— its magnificent, reckless profusion of fantasy— could not but be bewildering to its first critics, who had to pronounce upon it before they had (as Ballested [1] would put it) acclimatised themselves to its atmosphere. Its reception, then, was much more dubious than that of *Brand* had been. We find even George Brandes writing of it: "What great and noble powers are wasted on this thankless material! Except in the fourth act, which has no connection with what goes before and after, and is witless in its satire, crude in its irony, and in its latter part scarcely comprehensible, there is almost throughout a wealth of poetry and a depth of thought such as we do not find, perhaps, in any of Ibsen's earlier works. . . . It would be unjust to deny that the book contains great beauties, or that it tells us all, and Norwegians in particular, some important truths; but beauties and truths are of far less value than beauty and truth in the singular, and Ibsen's poem is neither beautiful nor true. Contempt for humanity and self-hatred make a bad foundation on which to build a poetic work. What an unlovely and distorting view of life this is! What acrid pleasure can a poet find in thus sullying human nature?"[2] The friendship between

[1] See *The Lady from the Sea.*
[2] Brandes: *Ibsen and Björnson*, p. 35. London, Heinemann, 1899. Except in regard to the fourth act, Dr. Brandes has, in the introduction to *Peer Gynt* in the German collected edition, recanted his early condemnation of the poem.

Brandes and Ibsen was at this time just beginning, and—much to Ibsen's credit—it appears to
have suffered no check by reason of this outspoken
pronouncement.

On the other hand, he resented deeply a criticism by Clemens Petersen, who seems to have been
at this time regarded as the æsthetic lawgiver of
Copenhagen. Why he should have done so is not
very clear; for Petersen professed to prefer *Peer
Gynt* to *Brand*, and his criticism on *Brand* Ibsen
had apparently accepted without demur. Most of
Petersen's article is couched in a very heavy philosophic idiom; but the following extract, though
it refers chiefly to *Brand*, may convey some idea
of his general objection to both poems:—" When
a poet, as Ibsen does in *Brand*, depicts an error,
a one-sidedness, which is from first to last presented in an imposing light, it is not sufficient
that he should eventually, through a piece of sen-
sational symbolism, let that one-sidedness go to
ruin, and it is not sufficient that in the last word
of the drama [1] he should utter the name of that
with which the one-sidedness should have blended
in order to become truth. If he throughout his
work shows us this error—in virtue of its
strength, if for no other reason—justifying itself
as against everything that comes in contact with
it, then it is not only in the character depicted that
something is lacking, but in the work of art itself. That something is the Ideal, without which
the work of art cannot take rank as poetry—the
Ideal which here, as so often in art, lies only in
the lighting of the picture, but which is nevertheless the saving, the uplifting element. It is to

[1] The last words are " deus caritatis."

poetry what devotion is to religion. . . . In *Peer Gynt*, as in *Brand*, the ideal is lacking. But this must be said rather less strongly of *Peer Gynt*. There is more fantasy, more real freedom of spirit, less strain and less violence in this poem than in *Brand*." The critic then speaks of *Peer Gynt* as being "full of riddles which are insoluble, because there is nothing in them at all." Peer's identification of the Sphinx with the Boyg (Act IV. Sc. 12) he characterises as "Tankesvindel"—thought-swindling, or, as we might say, juggling with thought. The general upshot of his considerations is that *Peer Gynt* belongs, with Goldschmidt's *Corsaren*, to the domain of polemical journalism. It "is not poetry, because in the transmutation of reality into art it falls halfway short of the demands both of art and of reality."

Petersen's review is noteworthy, not for its own sake, but for the effect it produced on Ibsen. His letters to Björnson on the subject are the most vivid and spontaneous he ever wrote. Björnson happened to be in Copenhagen when Petersen's article appeared in *Fœdrelandet*, and Ibsen seems somehow to have blamed him for not preventing its appearance. "All I reproach you with," he says, "is inaction." But Petersen he accuses of lack of "loyalty," of "an intentional crime against truth and justice." "There is a lie involved in Clemens Petersen's article, not in what he says, but in what he refrains from saying. And he intentionally refrains from saying a great deal. . . . Tell me, now, is Peer Gynt himself not a personality, complete and individual? *I* know that he is. And the mother; is she not?"

But the most memorable passage in this memorable letter is the following piece of splendid arrogance: " My book *is* poetry; and if it is not, then it will be. The conception of poetry in our country, in Norway, shall be made to conform to the book." It certainly seems that any definition of poetry which should be so framed as to exclude *Peer Gynt* must have something of what Petersen himself called " Tankesvindel" about it.

Ibsen's burst of indignation relieved his mind, and three weeks later we find him writing, half apologetically, of the " cargo of nonsense " he had " shipped off " to Björnson, immediately on reading Petersen's review. He even sends a friendly " greeting" to the offending critic. But this is his last (published) letter to Björnson for something like fifteen years. How far the reception of *Peer Gynt* may have contributed to the breach between them, I do not know. Björnson's own criticism of the poem, as we shall presently see, was very favourable.

Peer Gynt was not, on its appearance, quite so popular as *Brand*. A second edition was called for in a fortnight; but the third edition did not appear until 1874, by which time the seventh edition of *Brand* was already on the market. Before the end of the century ten editions of *Peer Gynt* had appeared in Copenhagen as against fourteen of *Brand*. The first German translation appeared in 1881, and the present English translation in 1892. A French translation, by Count Prozor, appeared in the *Nouvelle Revue* in 1896, but does not seem to have been published in book form.

After a great deal of discussion as to the stage-

arrangement, *Peer Gynt*, largely abbreviated, was
produced, with Edvard Grieg's now famous in-
cidental music, at the Christiania Theatre in February 1876, Henrik Klausen playing the title-part.
It was acted thirty-seven times; but a fire which
destroyed some of the scenery put a stop to the
performances. In 1892, at the same theatre, the
first three acts were revived, with Björn Björnson
as Peer, and repeated fifty times. In the reper-
tory of the National Theatre, too (opened in
1899), *Peer Gynt* has taken a prominent place.
It was first given in 1902, and has up to the present (1906) been performed eighty-four times. In
the version which has established itself on the
Norwegian stage, all five acts are given, but the
fourth and fifth acts are greatly abbreviated. In
the season of 1886 the play was produced at the
Dagmar Theatre, Copenhagen. August Lind-
berg's Swedish Company acted it in Gothenburg
in 1892, in Stockholm in 1895, and afterwards
toured with it in Norway and Sweden. Count
Prozor's translation was acted by " L'Œuvre " at
the Nouveau Théâtre, Paris, in November, 1896,
of which remarkable production a lively account
by Mr. Bernard Shaw may be found in the *Saturday Review* of that period. At the Deutsches
Volkstheater in Vienna, in May 1902, two performances of *Peer Gynt* were given by the " Aka-
demisch-Litterarische Verein." I can find no
record of any other German production of the
play. The first production in the English language took place at the Grand Opera House, Chi-
cago, on October 29, 1906, when Mr. Richard
Mansfield appeared as Peer Gynt. Mr. Mansfield would seem to have acted the greater part

of the play, but to have omitted the Sæter-Girl
scene and the madhouse scene.

We have seen that the name, Peer Gynt, was
suggested to Ibsen by a folk-tale in Asbjörnsen
and Moe's invaluable collection. It is one of a
group of tales entitled *Reindeer-Hunting in the
Rondë Hills;*[1] and in the same group occurs the
adventure of Gudbrand Glesnë on the Gendin-
Edge, which Peer Gynt works up so unblushingly
in Act I., Sc. 1. The text of both these tales will
be found in the Appendix, and the reader will
recognise how very slight are the hints which set
the poet's imagination to work. The encounter
with the Sæter-Girls (Act II., Sc. 3), and the
struggle with the Boyg (Act II., Sc. 7) are fore-
shadowed in Asbjörnsen, and the concluding remark of Anders Ulsvolden evidently suggested to
Ibsen the idea of incarnating Fantasy in Peer
Gynt, as in Brand he had given us incarnate Will.
But the Peer Gynt of the drama has really nothing in common with the Peer Gynt of the story,
and the rest of the characters are not even re-
motely suggested. Many scattered traits and allusions, however, are borrowed from other legends
in the same storehouse of grotesque and marvellous imaginings. Thus the story of the devil
in a nutshell (Act I., Sc. 3) figures in Asbjörnsen under the title of *The Boy and the Devil.*[2]
The appearance of the Green-Clad One with her
Ugly Brat, who offers Peer Gynt a goblet of beer

---

[1] *Norske Huldre-Eventyr og Folkesagn*, Christiania, 1848,
p. 47. See also Copenhagen edition, 1896, p. 163.
[2] *Norske Folke-og Huldre-Eventyr*, Copenhagen, 1896, p. 48.

(Act III., Sc. 3), is obviously suggested by an incident in *Berthe Tuppenhaug's Stories.*[1] Old Berthe, too, supplies the idea of correcting Peer Gynt's eyesight according to the standard of the hill-trolls (Act II., Sc. 6), as well as the germ of the fantastic thread-ball episode in the last Act (Sc. 6). The castle, " East of the Sun and West of the Moon " (Act III., Sc. 4), gives its title to one of Asbjörnsen's stories,[2] which may be read in English in Mr. Andrew Lang's *Blue Fairy Book;* and " Soria Moria Castle " is the title of another legend.[3] Herr Passarge (in his *Henrik Ibsen,* Leipzig, 1883) goes so far as to trace the idea of Peer Gynt's shrinking from the casting-ladle, even though hell be the alternative (Act V., Sc. 7, &c.), to Asbjörnsen's story of *The Smith whom they Dared not let into Hell;*[4] but the circumstances are so different, and Ibsen's idea is such an inseparable part of the ethical scheme of the drama, that we can scarcely take it to have been suggested by this (or any other) individual story.[5] At the same time there is no doubt that *The Folk-Lore of Peer Gynt* might form the subject of a much more extended study than our

[1] *Ibid.*, p. 129.
[2] *Ibid.*, p. 259.
[3] Not included in the Copenhagen edition. See edition, Christiania, 1866, p. 115. See also Sir George Webbe Dasent's *Popular Tales from the Norse,* Edinburgh, 1859 ; new ed. 1903, p. 396. More or less representative selections from the storehouse of Asbjörnsen and Moe may also be found in *Tales from the Fjeld,* by G. W. Dasent, London, 1874, and in *Round the Yule Log,* by H. L. Brækstad, London, 1881.
[4] Copenhagen ed. 1896, p. 148.
[5] In this story, however, he probably found the suggestion of the " cross-roads " which figure so largely in the fifth act. In Asbjörnsen, they are explicitly stated to be the point where the ways to Heaven and Hell diverge.

space or our knowledge admits of.[1] The whole atmosphere of the first three acts and of the fifth is
that of the Norwegian Folk and Fairy Tales.
It must be remembered, too, that in the early
'sixties Ibsen was commissioned by the Norwegian
Government to visit Romsdal and Söndmöre for
the purpose of collecting folk-songs and legends.
To these journeys, no doubt, we are mainly indebted for the local colour of *Brand* and *Peer
Gynt*.

What are we to say now of the drift, the interpretation of *Peer Gynt?* The first and most
essential thing may be said in Ibsen's own words.
On February 24, 1868, he wrote from Rome to
Frederik Hegel: "I learn that the book has created much excitement in Norway. This does not
trouble me in the least; but both there and in
Denmark they have discovered much more satire
in it than was intended by me. Why can they not
read the book as a poem? For as such I wrote
it. The satirical passages are tolerably isolated.

[1] Further gleanings of legendary lore concerning Peer Gynt
may be found in the Norwegian periodical *Syn og Segn*, 1903,
pp. 119-130.   The writer, Per Aasmundstad, is of opinion that
Peer Gynt's real name was Peer Haagaa (the owner of Haagaa
farm) and that Gynt was either a name given him by the
huldra-folk, or else a local nickname for humorists of his kind.
According to this authority, he probably lived as far back as
the seventeenth century.   Per Aasmundstad's article is written
in the local dialect, with such ruthless phonetic accuracy that
I read it with difficulty; but he does not seem to have discovered anything that has a definite bearing on Ibsen's work.
From the wording of Ibsen's letters to Hegel, however (p. viii),
it would seem that he had some knowledge of the Gynt legend
over and above what was to be found in Asbjörnsen.   (For
access to *Syn og Segn*, and for other obliging assistance, I am
indebted to Herr Halvdan Koht, the author of the excellent
biographical introduction to Ibsen's Letters.)

But if the Norwegians of the present time recognise themselves, as it would appear they do, in the character of Peer Gynt, that is the good people's own affair." In the last sentence the innocence of intention is, no doubt, a little overdone; but there is still less doubt that Ibsen was absolutely sincere in declaring that he wrote it primarily as a poem, a work of pure imagination, and that as a work of pure imagination it ought primarily to be read. There is undeniably an undercurrent of ethical and satirical meaning in the play; but no one can properly enjoy or value it who is not swept along irresistibly by the surface stream of purely poetic invention and delineation. Peer himself is a character-creation on the heroic scale, as vital a personality as Falstaff or Don Quixote. It is here that the poem (as Clemens Petersen vaguely discerned) has a marked advantage over its predecessor. In spite of the tremendous energy with which he is depicted, Brand remains an abstraction or an attitude, rather than a human being. But Peer Gynt is human in every fibre—too human to be alien to any one of us. We know him, we understand him, we love him—for who does not love a genial, imaginative, philosophic rascal? As for his adventures and vicissitudes, if they do not give us pleasure in and for themselves, quite apart from any symbolic sub-intention—just as the adventures of Sindbad, or Gil Blas, or Tom Jones, or Huckleberry Finn give us pleasure—then assuredly the poem does not affect us as Ibsen intended that it should. Readers who approach it for the first time may therefore be counselled to pay no heed to its ethical or political meanings, and to take it as it

comes, simply as a dramatic romance or phan-
tasmagoria of purely human humour and pathos.
Reading it in this way, they will naturally find
a good deal that seems obscure and arbitrary; but
much of this will be cleared up on a second reading, by the aid of such sidelights as this Introduction can afford. No assiduity of study, however, can find in *Peer Gynt* a clear, consistent,
cut-and-dried allegory, with a place for everything
and everything in its place. It is not an allegory,
but (as aforesaid) a phantasmagory. This is
what the early critics did not realise. They quar-
relled with it for the very luxuriance of its invention, the buoyant irrepressible whimsicality
of its humour, the shimmering iridescence of its
style. They stood before an "undulant and di-
verse" carnival-pageant, and grumbled because
it would not fit into any recognised form, sanc-
tioned by their preconceived æsthetic principles.

I am far from maintaining that the reckless,
elusive capriciousness of the poem is an unmixed
merit. It would probably have done no harm if,
after the first rapture of composition had died
away, Ibsen had gone over it and pruned it a little
here and there. I can by no means endorse the
critics' sweeping condemnation of the fourth act,
which contains some of the most delightful passages in the whole poem; but the first scene of
this act is unquestionably shallow in conception
and diffuse in style—a piece of satiric journalism
rather than of literature. The concluding scenes
of the last act, too, would certainly have been none
the worse of a little compression. The auction
scene (Act V. Sc. 4), though it has a sort of fantastic impressiveness, seems to me hopelessly baf-

fling in its relation both to the outward story and to the inner significance of the poem. Here, and perhaps at some half-dozen other points, one may admit that Ibsen appears to have let his fancy run away with him; but the inert, excessive, or utterly enigmatic passages in *Peer Gynt* are surely few and brief in comparison with the passages in *Faust* to which the same epithets may be applied. On the other hand, the scenes of poignant and thrilling and haunting poetry are too many to be severally indicated. The first act, with its inimitable life and movement, Åse's death-scene, and the Pastor's speech in the last act, are usually cited as the culminating points of the poem; and there can be no doubt that Åse's death-scene, at any rate, is one of the supreme achievements of modern drama.[1] But there are several other scenes that I would place scarcely, if at all, lower than these. In point of weird intensity, there is nothing in the poem more marvellous than the Sæter-Girl scene (Act II. Sc. 3); in point of lyric movement, Peer Gynt's repudiation of Ingrid (Act II. Sc. 1) is incomparable; and in point of sheer beauty and pathos, Solveig's arrival at the hut (Act III. Sc. 3), with the whole of the scene that follows, stands supreme.[2] For my own part, I reckon the shipwreck scenes at the beginning of the fifth Act among the most impressive, as they are certainly not the least characteristic, in the poem. And, in enumerating its

---

[1] It is pretty clear that the poet designed Åse's death as a deliberate contrast to the death of Brand's mother.

[2] In all these remarks I have in mind, of course, the scenes in their original form. The reader will easily understand the loss which they inevitably suffer in being deprived of the crowning grace of richly-elaborated rhyme.

traits of undeniable greatness, one must by no
means forget the character of Åse, on which Ibsen
himself dwelt with justified complacency. There
is not a more life-like creation in the whole range
of drama.

Having now warned the reader against allowing
the search for symbolic or satiric meanings to
impair his enjoyment of the pure poetry of *Peer
Gynt*, I may proceed to point out some of the im-
plications which do indubitably underlie the surface aspects of the poem. These meanings fall
under three heads. First, we have universal-
human satire and symbolism, bearing upon human
nature in general, irrespective of race or nation-
ality. Next we have satire upon Norwegian human nature in particular, upon the religious and
political life of Norway as a nation. Lastly, we
find a certain number of local and ephemeral references—what, in the slang of our stage, are called
" topical allusions."

In order to provide the reader with a clue to
the complex meanings of *Peer Gynt*, on its higher
lines or planes of significance, I cannot do better
than quote some paragraphs from the admirable
summary of the drama given by Mr. P. H. Wicksteed in his *Four Lectures on Henrik Ibsen*.[1] Mr.
Wicksteed is in such perfect sympathy with Ibsen
in the stage of his development marked by *Brand*
and *Peer Gynt*, that he has understood these
poems, in my judgment, at least as well as any
other commentator, whether German or Scandi-
navian. He writes as follows:

" In *Brand* the hero is an embodied protest
against the poverty of spirit and half-heartedness

[1] London: Sonnenschein, 1892.

that Ibsen rebelled against in his countrymen. In *Peer Gynt* the hero is himself the embodiment of that spirit. In *Brand* the fundamental antithesis, upon which, as its central theme, the drama is constructed, is the contrast between the spirit of compromise on the one hand, and the motto ' everything or nothing ' on the other. And Peer Gynt is the very incarnation of a compromising dread of decisive committal to any one course. In *Brand* the problem of self-realisation and the relation of the individual to his surroundings is obscurely struggling for recognition, and in *Peer Gynt* it becomes the formal theme upon which all the fantastic variations of the drama are built up. In both plays alike the problems of heredity and the influence of early surroundings are more than touched upon; and both alike culminate in the doctrine that the only redeeming power on earth or in heaven is the power of love.

" Peer Gynt, as already stated, stands for the Norwegian people, much as they are sketched in *Brand*, though with more brightness of colouring. Hence his perpetual ' hedging ' and determination never so to commit himself that he cannot draw back. Hence his fragmentary life of smatterings. Hence his perpetual brooding over the former grandeur of his family, his idle dreams of the future, and his neglect of every present duty. Hence his deep-rooted selfishness and cynical indifference to all higher motives; and hence, above all, his sordid and superstitious religion; for to him religion is the apotheosis of the art of ' hedging.'

" But Ibsen's allegories are never stiffly or pedantically worked out. His characters, though typical, are personal. We could read *Brand,* and could feel the tragedy and learn the lessons of the drama without any knowledge whatever of the circumstances or feelings under which it was written, or the references to the Norwegian character and conduct with which it teems.

"So, too, with *Peer Gynt.* We may forget the national significance of the sketch, except where special allusions recall it to our minds, and may think only of the universal problems with which the poem deals, and which will retain their awful interest when Ibsen's polemic against his countrymen has sunk into oblivion. The study of *Peer Gynt* as an occasional poem should be strictly subsidiary and introductory to its study as the tragedy of a lost soul.

"What is it to be one's self? God *meant something* when he made each one of us. For a man to embody that meaning of God in his words and deeds, and so become in his degree a 'word of God made flesh,' is to be himself. But thus to be himself he must slay himself. That is to say, he must slay the craving to make himself the centre round which others revolve, and must strive to find his true orbit and swing, self-poised, round the great central light. But what if a poor devil can never puzzle out what on earth God *did* mean when he made him? Why, then, he must *feel* it. But how often your 'feeling' misses fire! Ay! there you have it. The devil has no stauncher ally than *want of perception!* [Act V., Sc. 9.]

"But, after all, you may generally find out what God meant you for, if you will face facts. It is easy to find a refuge from facts in lies, in

self-deception and in self-sufficiency. It is easy
to take credit to yourself for what circumstances
have done for you, and lay upon circumstances
what you owe to yourself. It is easy to think
you are realising yourself by refusing to become
a 'pack-horse for the weal and woe of others'
[Act IV., Sc. 1], keeping alternatives open and
never closing a door behind you or burning your
ships, and so always remaining the master of the
situation and self-possessed. If you choose to do
these easy things you may always 'get round'
your difficulties [Act II., Sc. 7], but you will
never get through them. You will remain master of the situation indeed, but the situation will
become poorer and narrower every day. If you
never commit yourself, you never express yourself, and your self becomes less and less significant
and decisive. Calculating selfishness is the anni-
hilation of self."

So far Mr. Wicksteed. The general significance
of the poem, in the terms of that theism which
may or may not have been Ibsen's personal creed
during the years of its incubation, could scarcely
be better expounded.

When we come to subsidiary meanings, we must
proceed more carefully, for we have the poet's own
word for it that many have been read into the
poem whereof he never dreamt. For example, in
his first letter to Björnson after reading Clemens
Petersen's criticism, he protested against that
critic's assumption that the Strange Passenger
(Act V., Scs. 1 & 2) was symbolic of "dread."
"If my head had been on the block," he said,
"and such an explanation would have saved my
life, it would never have occurred to me. I never

thought of such a thing. I stuck in the scene as
a mere caprice." For this element of caprice
we must always allow. The whole fourth act,
the poet told the present writer, was an after-
thought, and did not belong to the original
scheme of the play.

Here we come upon the question whether Ibsen
consciously designed *Peer Gynt* as a counterblast
to Björnson's idyllic peasant-novel, *Synnöve Solbakken.* This theory, put forward by a judicious
French critic, M. Auguste Ehrhard,[1] among
others, has always seemed to me very far-fetched;
but as Dr. Brandes, in the introduction to *Peer
Gynt* in the German collected edition, appears to
give it his sanction, I quote what he says on
the point: " German critics have laid special
emphasis on the fact that Ibsen here placed himself in conscious opposition to Björnson's glorifi-
cation, in his early novels, of the younger gener-
ation of Norwegian peasants. Quarrelsomeness
and love of fighting were represented in Thorb-
jörn, the hero of *Synnöve Solbakken,* as traits
of the traditional old-Norse viking spirit; in
Arne the poetic proclivities of the people were
placed in an engaging light. The vaunted fis-
ticuff-heroism was, in Ibsen's view, nothing but
rawness, and the poetic proclivities of Norwegian youth appeared to him, in the last anal-
ysis, simply a very prevalent love of lying and
gasconading. The Norwegians appear in the
caricaturing mirror of this brilliant poem as a
people who, in smug contentment, are ' to themselves enough,' and therefore laud everything that
is their own, however insignificant it may be,

[1] *Henrik Ibsen et le Théâtre Contemporain.* Paris, 1892.

shrink from all decisive action, and have for their national vice a tendency to fantastication and braggadocio." That *Peer Gynt* is a counterblast to national romanticism and chauvinism in general there can of course be no doubt; but I see no reason to suppose that Ibsen had Björnson's novels specially in view, or intended anything like a "caricature" of them. It is pretty clear, too, that Björnson himself had no such idea in his mind when he reviewed the poem in the *Norsk Folkeblad* for November 23, 1867. His long article is almost entirely laudatory, and certainly shows no smallest sign of hostile party-spirit. "*Peer Gynt*," says Björnson, "is a satire upon Norwegian egoism, narrowness, and self-sufficiency, so executed as to have made me not only again and again laugh till I was sore, but again and again give thanks to the author in my heart —as I here do publicly." Beyond remarking upon the over-exuberance of detail, and criticising the versification, Björnson says little or nothing in dispraise of the poem. On the other hand he says curiously little of its individual beauties. He never mentions Åse, says nothing of her death-scene, or of the Pastor's speech, and picks out as the best thing in the play the thread-ball scene (Act V., Sc. 6).

The most obviously satirical passage of the first three acts is the scene in the Dovrë-King's palace (Act II., Sc. 6), with its jibe at Norwegian national vanity:

> The cow gives cakes and the bullock mead
> Ask not if its taste be sour or sweet;
> The main matter is, and you mustn't forget it,
> It's all of it home-brewed.

Much more difficult is the interpretation of the Boyg,[1] that vague, shapeless, ubiquitous, inevitable, invulnerable Thing which Peer encounters in the following scene (Act II., Sc. 7). Ibsen found it in the folk-tale, and was attracted, no doubt, by the sheer uncanniness and eerieness of the idea. Neither can one doubt, however, that in his own mind he attributed to the monster some symbolic signification. Dr. Brandes would have us see in it the Spirit of Compromise—the same evil spirit which is assailed in *Brand*. The Swedish critic, Vasenius, interprets it as Peer Gynt's own consciousness of his inability to take a decisive step—to go through an obstacle in place of skirting round it. Herr Passarge reads in it a symbol of the mass of mankind, *perpetuum immobile*, opposing its sheer force of inertia to every forward movement.[2] This would make it nearly equivalent to " the compact majority " of *An Enemy of the People;* or, looking at it from a slightly different angle, we might see in the scene an illustration in action of that despairing cry of Schiller's Talbot: " Mit der Dummheit kämpfen

1 Deeming it unnecessary to trouble our readers with niceties of pronunciation, we have represented the " Böig " of the original by the more easily pronouncible " Boyg." The root-idea seems to be that of bending, of sinuousness ; compare Norwegian *böie*, German *biegen*, to bend. In Aasmundstad's version of the *Peer Gynt* legends (see Note, p. xvii) when the Boyg names itself, Peer answers " Antel du æ rak hell bògjë, saa fæ du sleppe mé fram "—" Whether you are straight or crooked, you must let me pass." The German translator, both in the folk-tale and in the drama, renders " Böigen " by " der Krumme." So far as we are aware, the name occurs in no other folk-tale save that of *Peer Gynt*. It is not generic, but denotes an individual troll-monster.

2 Dr. A. von Hanstein (*Ibsen als Idealist*, Leipzig, 1897, p. 67), states that Ibsen himself endorsed this interpretation ; but I do not know on what evidence his statement is founded.

Götter selbst vergebens." The truth probably is
that the poet vaguely intended this vague monster to be as elusive in its symbolism as in its
physical constitution. But when, in Act IV., Sc.
12, he formally identifies the Boyg with the
Sphinx, we may surely conclude that one of the
interpretations present to his mind was metaphy-
sical. In this aspect, the Boyg would typify the
riddle of existence, with which we grapple in vain,
and which we have to " get round " as best we can.

The fourth act contains a good many special
allusions, in addition to the general, and somewhat crude, satire in the opening scene on the
characteristics of different nationalities, with
particular reference to their conduct in the Dano-
German crisis. Peer's dreams of African colo-
nisation (Act IV., Sc. 5) are said to refer to certain projects which Ole Bull had about this time
been ventilating. But it is especially in the madhouse scene (Act IV., Sc. 13) that satiric sallies
abound. " The Fellah with the royal mummy on
his back," says Henrik Jæger,[1] " is—like Trumpeterstråle—a cut at the Swedes, the mummy being Charles the Twelfth. Like the Fellah, it is
implied, the Swedes are extremely proud of their
'Hero-king,' and yet during the Dano-German
war they showed not the smallest sign of having
anything in common with him, unless it were
that they, like him, 'kept still and completely
dead.' In the delusion of the minister Hussein,
who imagines himself a pen, there is a general
reference to the futile address- and note-monger-
ing which went on in Norwegian-Swedish official-

[1] *Henrik Ibsen*, 1828–1888. *Et Literært Livsbillede*, Copenhagen, 1888. English Translation, London, Heinemann, 1890.

dom during the Dano-German War, and a more
special one to an eminent Swedish statesman
[Grev Manderström], who, during the war, had
been extremely proud of his official notes, and
had imagined that by means of them he might
exercise a decisive influence on the course of
events."

Most prominent and unmistakable of all the
satiric passages, however, is the attack on the
language-reformers in the personage of Huhu.
In the list of characters, Huhu is set down as a
" Målstræver from Zanzibar." Now the Mål-
strævers are a party which desires to substitute
a language compounded from the various local
dialects for the Norwegian of the townsfolk and
of literature. This they call Danish, and declare
to be practically a foreign tongue to the peasants,
who form the backbone of the Norwegian nation.
Ibsen's satire, it must be said, has had little or
no effect on the movement, which has gone on
slowly but steadily, and has of late years met
with official and legislative recognition. There
is a large and increasing literature in the " Mål ";
it is taught in schools and it is spoken in the
Storthing. Where the movement may end it is
hard to say. It must seem to a foreigner, as it
seemed to Ibsen, retrograde and obscurantist;
but there is doubtless some genuine impulse behind it which the foreigner cannot appreciate.

The principles which have guided us in the following transcript demand a few words of explanation. *Peer Gynt* is written from first to last
in rhymed verse. Six or eight different measures
are employed in the various scenes, and the

rhymes are exceedingly rich and complex. The frequency of final light syllables in Norwegian implies an exceptional abundance of double rhymes, and Ibsen has taken full advantage of this peculiarity. In the short first scene of the second act, for example, twenty-five out of the forty lines end in double rhymes, and there are three double-rhymed triplets. The tintinnabulation of these double rhymes, then, gives to most of the scenes a metrical character which it might puzzle Mr. Swinburne himself to reproduce in English. Moreover, the ordinary objections to rhymed translations seemed to apply with exceptional force in the case of *Peer Gynt*. The characteristic quality of its style is its vernacular ease and simplicity. It would have been heartbreaking work (apart from its extreme difficulty) to substitute for this racy terseness the conventional graces of English poetic diction, padding here and perverting there. To a prose translation, on the other hand, the objections seemed even greater. It is possible to give in prose some faint adumbration of epic dignity; but we had here no epic to deal with. We found (though the statement may at first seem paradoxical) that the same vernacular simplicity of style which forbade a translation in rhyme, was no less hostile to a translation in prose. The characteristic quality of the poet's achievement lay precisely in his having, by the aid of rhythm and rhyme, transfigured the most easy and natural dialogue, without the least sacrifice of its naturalness. Entirely to eliminate these graces of form would have been to reduce the poem to prose indeed. It seemed little better than casting a silver statue

into the crucible and asking the world to divine
from the ingot something of the sculptor's power.
A prose translation, in short, could not but strip
Fantasy of its pinions, rob Satire of its barbs.
The poet himself, moreover, expressly declared
that he would rather let *Peer Gynt* remain untranslated than see it rendered in prose. After
a good deal of reflection and experiment, we
finally suggested to him a middle course between
prose and rhyme: a translation as nearly as possible in the metres of the original, but with the
rhymes suppressed. To this compromise he as-
sented, and the following pages are the result.

We had no precedent—within our knowledge,
at any rate—to guide us, and were forced to lay
down our own laws. Even at the risk of falling
between two stools, we proposed to ourselves a
dual purpose. We sought to produce a translation
which should convey to the general reader some
faint conception of the movement and colour, the
wit and pathos, of the original, and at the same
time a transcript which should serve the student
as a "crib" to the Norwegian text. This, then,
the reader must be good enough to bear in mind:
that the following version is designed to facili-
tate, not to supersede, the study of the original.
But, apart from our desire to provide a "crib"
to *Peer Gynt*, we felt that, in taking the liberty of
suppressing the rhymes, we abjured our right to
any other liberty whatsoever. A rhymed paraphrase of a great poem may have a beauty of its
own; an unrhymed version must be no paraphrase, but a faithful transcript, else "the rip-
ple of laughing rhyme" has been sacrificed in
vain. Our fundamental principle, then, has been

to represent the original *line for line;* and to this
principle we have adhered with the utmost fidel-
ity. There are probably not fifty cases in the
whole poem in which a word has been transferred
from one line to another, and then only some pro-
noun or auxiliary verb. It is needless to say that
in adhering to this principle we have often had to
resist temptation. Many cases presented themselves in which greater clearness, grace, and vigour
might easily have been attained by transferring
a word or phrase from this line to that, or even
altering the sequence of a whole group of lines.
In no case have we yielded to such temptation,
feeling that, our rule once relaxed, we should in-
sensibly but inevitably lapse into mere paraphrase. Temptation beset us with especial force
in the less vital passages of the poem. In these
places it would have been easy to give our rendering some approach to grace and point by dis-
regarding inversions and other defects of expression, justified in the original by the wit and spirit
of the rhymes, but of course deprived in our transcript of any such excuse. Here, as elsewhere, we
were proof against temptation; it is for our
readers to decide whether our constancy was
heroic or pedantic.

It would be folly to pretend either that we have
reproduced every word of the original, or that
we have avoided all necessity for "padding."
The chief drawback of our line-for-line principle
is that it has debarred us from eking out the de-
ficiency of one line with the superfluity of the
next. We trust, however, that few essential ideas,
or even words, of the original will be found quite
unaccounted for; while with regard to padding,

we have tried, where we found it absolutely
forced upon us, to use only such mechanical parts
of speech as introduced no new idea into the con-
text. We have found by experiment that the fact
of writing in measure has frequently enabled us
to keep much closer to the original than would
have been possible in prose. This is not in reality so strange as it may at first sight appear. A
prose translation of verse can avoid paraphrase
only at the cost of grotesque inelegance; whereas
in rendering metre into metre, we are working
under the same laws which govern the original,
and are therefore enabled in many cases to adopt
identical forms of expression, which would be
quite inadmissible in prose.

Thirty out of the thirty-eight scenes into which
the five acts are divided are written almost entirely in an irregular measure of four accents,
evidently designed to give the greatest possible
variety and suppleness to the dialogue. The four
accents constitute almost the only assignable law
of this measure, the feet being of any length,
from two to four syllables, and of all possible de-
nominations—iambics, trochees, dactyls, ana-
pæsts, amphibrachs. The effect is at first rather
baffling to the unaccustomed ear; but when one
gets into the swing of the rub-a-dub rhythm, if
we may venture to call it so, the feeling of rug-
gedness vanishes, and the verse is found to be
capable of poignantly pathetic, as well as of buoy-
antly humorous, expression.

We have not attempted to reproduce each line
of this measure accurately, foot for foot, holding
it enough to observe the law of the four accents.
Where the four-accent rule is obviously departed

from, it will generally be found to be in obedience
to the original; for Ibsen now and then (but very
rarely) introduces a line or couplet of three or of
five accents.

Of the eight scenes in which this measure is not
employed, three—Act I. Sc. 1, Act II. Sc. 1,
and Act IV. Sc. 7—are in a perfectly regular
trochaic measure of four accents, the lines con-
taining seven or eight syllables, according as the
rhymes are single or double. In dealing with
this measure, we have not thought it necessary
to follow the precise arrangement of the original
in the alternation of seven and eight syllable
lines. In other words, we have sometimes represented a seven-syllable line by one of eight syllables, an eight-syllable line by one of seven. In
the short first scene of the second act, however,
every line represents accurately the length of the
corresponding line in the original.

The fourth scene of Act II. is written in lines
of three accents; the last scene of the third act—
Åse's death-scene—in lines of three accents with
alternate double and single rhymes. In rendering this scene, we have been careful to preserve
the alternation of strong with light endings,
which gives it its metrical character.

Two scenes—Act IV. Sc. 1, and Act V. Sc. 2—
consist of four-accent iambic lines, differing from
the octosyllabic verse of *Marmion* or *The Giaour*
chiefly in the greater prevalence of double and
even treble rhymes. Finally, the sixth scene of
Act V. consists mainly of eight-line lyrical stan-
zas, with two accents in each line, Peer Gynt's
interspersed remarks being in trochaic verses, like
those of Act I., Sc. 1. In such intercalated pas-

sages, so to speak, as the rhapsodies of Huhu
and the Fellah in Act IV., Sc. 13, and the Pastor's speech at the grave in Act V., Sc. 3, we
have accurately reproduced the measures of the
original. The Pastor's speech is the only passage
in the whole poem which is couched in iambic
decasyllables.

In dealing with idioms and proverbial expres-
sions, our practice has not been very consistent.
We have sometimes, where they seemed pecu-
liarly racy and expressive, translated them literally; in other cases we have had recourse to the
nearest English equivalent, even where the meta-
phor employed is quite different. In the latter
instances we have usually given the literal rendering of the phrase in a footnote.

For the present edition the text has been carefully revised, and some rough edges have, it is
hoped, been smoothed away; but no very essential
alteration has been made. While we are keenly
conscious of all that the poem loses in our rendering, we cannot but feel that it has justified its
existence, inasmuch as it has brought home to
thousands of readers on both sides of the Atlantic
a not wholly inadequate sense of the greatness of
the original.

W. A.

PEER GYNT

(1867)

CHARACTERS.

ÅSE,[1] *a peasant's widow.*

PEER GYNT,[2] *her son.*

TWO OLD WOMEN *with corn-sacks.* ASLAK, *a smith.*
    WEDDING GUESTS. A KITCHEN-MASTER, A FIDDLER,
    ETC.

A MAN AND WIFE, *newcomers to the district.*

SOLVEIG and LITTLE HELGA, *their daughters.*

THE FARMER AT HEGSTAD.

INGRID, *his daughter.*

THE BRIDEGROOM and HIS PARENTS.

THREE SÆTER-GIRLS. A GREEN-CLAD WOMAN.

THE OLD MAN OF THE DOVRË.

A TROLL-COURTIER. SEVERAL OTHERS. TROLL-
    MAIDENS and TROLL-URCHINS. A COUPLE OF
    WITCHES. BROWNIES, NIXIES, GNOMES, ETC.

AN UGLY BRAT. A VOICE IN THE DARKNESS. BIRD-
    CRIES.

KARI, *a cottar's wife.*

Master COTTON, Monsieur BALLON, Herren VON
    EBERKOPF and TRUMPETERSTRÅLE, *gentlemen on
    their travels.* A THIEF and A RECEIVER.

ANITRA, *daughter of a Bedouin chief.*

ARABS, FEMALE SLAVES, DANCING-GIRLS, ETC.

THE MEMNON-STATUE (*singing*). THE SPHINX AT
    GIZEH (*muta persona*).

PROFESSOR BEGRIFFENFELDT, Dr. phil., *director of the
    madhouse at Cairo.*

HUHU, *a language-reformer from the coast of Malabar.*
    HUSSEIN, *an eastern Minister.* A FELLAH, *with a
    royal mummy.*

SEVERAL MADMEN, with their KEEPERS.

A NORWEGIAN SKIPPER and HIS CREW. A STRANGE
    PASSENGER.

A PASTOR. A FUNERAL-PARTY. A PARISH-OFFICER.
    A BUTTON-MOULDER. A LEAN PERSON.

(*The action, which opens in the beginning of the present
[that is the nineteenth] century, and ends towards our own
days [1867], takes place partly in Gudbrandsdale, and on
the mountains around it, partly on the coast of Morocco, in
the desert of Sahara, in a madhouse at Cairo, at sea, etc.*)

[1] Pronounce *Oasë.* The letter *å* is pronounced like the *o* in
"home."

[2] Pronounce *Pair Günt*—the *G* hard, the *y* like the German
modified *ü.*

PEER GYNT.

ACT FIRST.

SCENE FIRST.

A wooded hillside near Åse's *farm. A river rushes
    down the slope. On the further side of it an old
    mill-shed. It is a hot day in summer.*

Peer Gynt, *a strongly-built youth of twenty, comes
    down the pathway. His mother,* Åse, *a small,
    slightly-built woman, follows him, scolding angrily.*

Åse.

Peer, you're lying!

Peer.

[*Without stopping.*]
No, I am not!

Åse.

Well then, swear that it is true!

Peer.

Swear? Why should I?

Åse.

See, you dare not!
It's a lie from first to last.

PEER.

[*Stopping.*]

It is true—each blessed word !

ÅSE.

[*Confronting him.*]

Don't you blush before your mother ?
First you skulk among the mountains
Monthlong in the busiest season,
Stalking reindeer in the snows ;
Home you come then, torn and tattered,
Gun amissing, likewise game ;—
And at last, with open eyes,
Think to get me to believe
All the wildest hunters'-lies !—
Well, where did you find the buck, then ?

PEER.

West near Gendin.[1]

ÅSE.

[*Laughing scornfully.*]

Ah !   Indeed .

PEER.

Keen the blast towards me swept ;
Hidden by an alder-clump,
He was scraping in the snow-crust
After lichen——

ÅSE.

[*As before.*]

Doubtless, yes !

PEER.

Breathlessly I stood and listened,

[1] Pronounce *Yendeen.*

Heard the crunching of his hoof,
Saw the branches of one antler.
Softly then among the boulders
I crept forward on my belly.
Crouched in the moraine I peered up;—
Such a buck, so sleek and fat,
You, I'm sure, have ne'er set eyes on.

ÅSE.

No, of course not!

PEER.

Bang! I fired.
Clean he dropped upon the hillside.
But the instant that he fell,
I sat firm astride his back,
Gripped him by the left ear tightly,
And had almost sunk my knife-blade
In his neck, behind his skull—
When, behold! the brute screamed wildly,
Sprang upon his feet like lightning,
With a back-cast of his head
From my fist made knife and sheath fly,
Pinned me tightly by the thigh,
Jammed his horns against my legs,
Clenched me like a pair of tongs;—
Then forthwith away he flew
Right along the Gendin-Edge!

ÅSE.

[*Involuntarily.*]

Jesus save us——!

PEER.

Have you ever
Chanced to see the Gendin-Edge?
Nigh on four miles long it stretches
Sharp before you like a scythe.

Down o'er glaciers, landslips, screes,
Down the toppling grey moraines,
You can see, both right and left,
Straight into the tarns that slumber,
Black and sluggish, more than seven
Hundred fathoms deep below you.
              Right along the Edge we two
Clove our passage through the air.
              Never rode I such a colt!
Straight before us as we rushed
'Twas as though there glittered suns.
Brown-backed eagles that were sailing
In the wide and dizzy void
Half-way 'twixt us and the tarns,
Dropped behind, like motes in air.
              On the shores crashed hurtling ice-floes,
But no echo reached my ears.
Only sprites of dizziness [1] sprang,
Dancing, round ;—they sang, they swung,
Circle-wise, past sight and hearing!

ÅSE.
[Dizzy.]

Oh, God save me!

PEER.
              All at once,
At a desperate, break-neck spot,
Rose a great cock-ptarmigan,
Flapping, cackling, terrified,
From the crack where he lay hidden
At the buck's feet on the Edge.
              Then the buck shied half around,

---

[1] This is the poet's own explanation of this difficult passage.
"Hvirvlens vætter," he writes, is equivalent to "Svimmelhedens
ånder"—*i.e.*, spirits of dizziness or vertigo.

Leapt sky-high, and down we plunged,
Both of us, into the depths !
   [Åse *totters, and catches at the trunk of a*
    tree. PEER GYNT *continues :*
 Mountain walls behind us, black,
And below a void unfathomed !
  First we clove through banks of mist,
Then we clove a flock of sea-gulls,
So that they, in mid-air startled,
Flew in all directions, screaming.
  Downward rushed we, ever downward.
But beneath us something shimmered,
Whitish, like a reindeer's belly.—
Mother, 'twas our own reflection
In the glass-smooth mountain tarn,
Shooting up towards the surface
With the same wild rush of speed
Wherewith we were shooting downwards.

Åse.

[Gasping for breath.]

Peer !   God help me—— !   Quickly, tell——

Peer.

Buck from over, buck from under,
In a moment clashed together,
Scattering foam-flecks all around.
  There we lay then, floating, plashing,—
But at last we made our way
Somehow to the northern shore ;
Swam the buck, I clung behind him :—
I ran homewards——

Åse.

But the buck, dear ?

PEER.

He's there still, for aught I know ;—

> [*Snaps his fingers, turns on his heel, and
>   adds :*

Catch him, and you're welcome to him !

ÅSE.

And your neck you haven't broken ?
Haven't broken both your thighs ?
And your backbone, too, is whole ?
Oh, dear Lord—what thanks, what praise,
Should be thine who helped my boy !
There's a rent, though, in your breeches ;
But it's scarce worth talking of
When one thinks what dreadful things
Might have come of such a leap——!

> [*Stops suddenly, looks at him open-mouthed
>   and wide-eyed; cannot find words for
>   some time, but at last bursts out :*

Oh, you devil's story-teller,
Cross of Christ, how you can lie !
All this screed you foist upon me,
I remember now, I knew it
When I was a girl of twenty.
Gudbrand Glesnë [1] it befell,
Never you, you——

PEER.

Me as well.
Such a thing can happen twice.

ÅSE.

[*Exasperated.*]

Yes, a lie, turned topsy-turvy,
Can be prinked and tinselled out,
Decked in plumage new and fine,

[1] See Appendix.

Till none knows its lean old carcass.
That is just what you've been doing,
Vamping up things, wild and grand,
Garnishing with eagles' backs
And with all the other horrors,
Lying right and lying left,
Filling me with speechless dread,
Till at last I recognised not
What of old I'd heard and known!

PEER.

If another talked like that
I'd half kill him for his pains.

Åse.
[*Weeping.*]
Oh, would God I lay a corpse;
Would the black earth held me sleeping.
Prayers and tears don't bite upon him.—
Peer, you're lost, and ever will be!

PEER.

Darling, pretty little mother,
You are right in every word;—
Don't be cross, be happy——

Åse.
                        Silence!

Could I, if I would, be happy,
With a pig like you for son?
Think how bitter I must find it,
I, a poor defenceless widow,
Ever to be put to shame!
                        [*Weeping again.*
How much have we now remaining
From your grandsire's days of glory?

Where are now the sacks[1] of coin
Left behind by Rasmus Gynt ?
Ah, your father lent them wings,—
Lavished them abroad like sand,
Buying land in every parish,
Driving round in gilded chariots.
Where is all the wealth he wasted
At the famous winter-banquet,
When each guest sent glass and bottle
Shivering 'gainst the wall behind him ?

PEER.

Where's the snow of yester-year ?

ÅSE.

Silence, boy, before your mother !
See the farmhouse !   Every second
Window-pane is stopped with clouts.
Hedges, fences, all are down,
Beasts exposed to wind and weather,
Fields and meadows lying fallow,
Every month a new distraint——

PEER.

Come now, stop this old-wife's talk !
Many a time has luck seemed drooping,
And sprung up as high as ever !

ÅSE.

Salt-strewn is the soil it grew from.
Lord, but you're a rare one, you,—
Just as pert and jaunty still,
Just as bold as when the Pastor,
Newly come from Copenhagen,
Bade you tell your Christian name,

Literally "bushels."

And declared that such a headpiece
Many a Prince down there might envy ;
Till the cob your father gave him,
With a sledge to boot, in thanks
For his pleasant, friendly talk.——
Ah, but things went bravely then !
Provost,[1] Captain, all the rest,
Dropped in daily, ate and drank,
Swilling, till they well-nigh burst.
But 'tis need that tests one's neighbour.
Lonely here it grew, and silent,
From the day that " Gold-bag Jon "[2]
Started with his pack, a pedlar.
　　　　　　　[*Dries her eyes with her apron.*
Ah, you're big and strong enough,
You should be a staff and pillar
For your mother's frail old age,—
You should keep the farm-work going,
Guard the remnants of your gear ;—
　　　　　　　　　　[*Crying again.*
Oh, God help me, small's the profit
You have been to me, you scamp !
Lounging by the hearth at home,
Grubbing in the charcoal embers ;
Or, round all the country, frightening
Girls away from merry-makings—
Shaming me in all directions,
Fighting with the worst rapscallions——

PEER.
[*Turning away from her.*]
Let me be.

[1] An ecclesiastical dignitary—something equivalent to a rural
dean.
[2] " Jon med Skjæppen "—literally, " John with the Bushel "
—a nickname given him in his days of prosperity, in allusion to
his supposed bushels of money.

ÅSE.

[*Following him.*]

Can you deny
That you were the foremost brawler
In the mighty battle royal
Fought the other day at Lundë,
When you raged like mongrels mad?
Who was it but you that broke
Blacksmith Aslak's arm for him,—
Or at any rate that wrenched one
Of his fingers out of joint?

PEER.

Who has filled you with such prate?

ÅSE.

[*Hotly.*]

Cottar Kari heard the yells!

PEER.

[*Rubbing his elbow.*]

Maybe, but 'twas I that howled.

ÅSE.

You?

PEER.

Yes, mother,—*I* got beaten.

ÅSE.

What d'you say?

PEER.

He's limber, he is.

ÅSE.

Who?

PEER.

Why Aslak, to be sure.

ÅSE.

Shame—and shame ; I spit upon you !
Such a worthless sot as that,
Such a brawler, such a sodden
Dram-sponge to have beaten you !
                              [*Weeping again.*
Many a shame and slight I've suffered ;
But that this should come to pass
Is the worst disgrace of all.
What if he be ne'er so limber,
Need you therefore be a weakling ?

PEER.

Though I hammer or am hammered,—
Still we must have lamentations.

                                [*Laughing*

Cheer up, mother——

ÅSE.

                    What ?   You're lying

Now again ?

PEER.

          Yes, just this once.
Come now, wipe your tears away ;—
                    [*Clenching his left hand.*
See,—with this same pair of tongs,
Thus I held the smith bent double,
While my sledge-hammer right fist——

ÅSE.

Oh, you brawler !   You will bring me
With your doings to the grave !

PEER.

No, you're worth a better fate;
Better twenty thousand times!
Little, ugly, dear old mother,
You may safely trust my word,—
All the parish shall exalt you;
Only wait till I have done
Something—something really grand .

Åse.

[*Contemptuously.*]

You!

PEER.

Who knows what may befall one

Åse.

Could you but find so much sense,
One day, as to do the darning
Of your breeches for yourself !

PEER.

[*Hotly.*]

I will be a king, a kaiser!

Åse

Oh, God comfort me, he's losing
All the little wits he'd left !

PEER.

Yes, I will !   Just give me time !

Åse.

Give you time, you'll be a prince,
So the saying goes, I think !

PEER.

You shall see!

ÅSE.

Oh, hold your tongue
You're as mad as mad can be.—
     Ah, and yet it's true enough,—
Something might have come of you,
Had you not been steeped for ever
In your lies and trash and moonshine.
Hegstad's girl was fond of you.
Easily you could have won her
Had you wooed her with a will——

PEER.

Could I ?

ÅSE.

     The old man's too feeble
Not to give his child her way.
He is stiff-necked in a fashion ;
But at last 'tis Ingrid rules ;
And where she leads, step by step
Stumps the gaffer, grumbling, after.
                    [*Begins to cry again.*
Ah, my Peer !—a golden girl—
Land entailed on her ! Just think,
Had you set your mind upon it,
You'd be now a bridegroom brave,—
You that stand here grimed and tattered !

PEER.
[*Briskly.*]
Come, we'll go a-wooing then !

ÅSE.

Where ?

PEER.

At Hegstad !

ÅSE.

Ah, poor boy;
Hegstad way is barred to wooers!

PEER.

How is that?

ÅSE.

Ah, woe is me!
Lost the moment, lost the luck——

PEER.

Speak!

ÅSE.

[*Sobbing.*]
While in the Wester-hills
You in air were riding reindeer,
Here Mads Moen's[1] won the girl!

PEER.

What! That women's-bugbear! He——

ÅSE.

Ay, she's taking him for husband.

PEER.

Wait you here till I have harnessed
Horse and waggon——   [*Going.*

ÅSE.

Spare your pains.
They are to be wed to-morrow——

PEER.

Pooh; this evening I'll be there!

[1] Pronounce *Maass-Moo-en.*

ÅSE.

Fie now !   Would you crown our miseries
With a load of all men's scorn ?

PEER.

Never fear ; 'twill all go well.
         [*Shouting and laughing at the same time.*
Mother, jump !   We'll spare the waggon ;
'Twould take time to fetch the mare up——
                  [*Lifts her up in his arms.*

ÅSE.

Put me down !

PEER.

               No, in my arms
I will bear you to the wedding !
                  [*Wades out into the stream.*

ÅSE.

Help !   The Lord have mercy on us !
Peer !   We're drowning——

PEER.

                        I was born
For a braver death——

ÅSE.

                  Ay, true ;
Sure enough you'll hang at last !
                  [*Tugging at his hair.*
Oh, you brute !

PEER.

            Keep quiet now ;
Here the bottom's slippery-slimy.

ÅSE.

Ass !

PEER.

That's right, don't spare your tongue;
That does no one any harm.
Now it's shelving up again——

ÅSE.

Don't you drop me!

PEER.

Heisan! Hop!
Now we'll play at Peer and reindeer;—

[*Curvetting.*

I'm the reindeer, you are Peer!

ÅSE.

Oh, I'm going clean distraught!

PEER.

See now—we have reached the shallows;—

[*Wades ashore.*

Come, a kiss now, for the reindeer;
Just to thank him for the ride——

ÅSE.

[*Boxing his ears.*]
This is how I thank him!

PEER.

Ow!

That's a miserable fare!

ÅSE.

Put me down!

PEER.

First to the wedding.

Be my spokesman.   You're so clever;
Talk to him, the old curmudgeon ;
Say Mads Moen's good for nothing——

Åse.

Put me down !

Peer.

    And tell him then
What a rare lad is Peer Gynt.

Åse.

Truly, you may swear to that !
Fine's the character I'll give you.
Through and through I'll show you up;
All about your devil's pranks
I will tell them straight and plain——

Peer.

Will you ?

Åse.

[Kicking with rage.]
    I won't stay my tongue
Till the old man sets his dog
At you, as you were a tramp !

Peer.

H'm ; then I must go alone.

Åse.

Ay, but I'll come after you !

Peer.

Mother dear, you haven't strength——

Åse.

Strength? When I'm in such a rage,
I could crush the rocks to powder!
Hu! I'd make a meal of flints!
Put me down!

Peer.

You'll promise then——

Åse.

Nothing! I'll to Hegstad with you!
They shall know you, what you are!

Peer.

Then you'll even have to stay here.

Åse.

Never! To the feast I'm coming!

Peer.

That you shan't.

Åse.

What will you do?

Peer.

Perch you on the mill-house roof.
        [*He puts her up on the roof.*   Åse *screams.*

Åse.

Lift me down!

Peer.

Yes, if you'll listen——

Åse.

Rubbish!

Peer.

Dearest mother, pray——

ÅSE.

[*Throwing a sod of grass at him.*]
Lift me down this moment, Peer!

PEER.

If I dared, be sure I would.   [*Coming nearer.*
Now remember, sit quite still.
Do not sprawl and kick about;
Do not tug and tear the shingles,—
Else 'twill be the worse for you;
You might topple down.

ÅSE.

You beast

PEER.

Do not kick!

ÅSE.

I'd have you blown,
Like a changeling, into space![1]

PEER.

Mother, fie!

ÅSE.

Bah

PEER.

Rather give your
Blessing on my undertaking.
Will you?   Eh?

ÅSE.

I'll thrash you soundly,
Hulking fellow though you be!

[1] It is believed in some parts of Norway that "changelings"
(elf-children left in the stead of those taken away by the fairies)
can, by certain spells, be made to fly away up the chimney.

PEER.

Well, good-bye then, mother dear !
Patience ; I'll be back ere long.
>   [*Is going, but turns, holds up his finger*
>   *warningly, and says :*
Careful now, don't kick and sprawl !   [*Goes.*

ÅSE.

Peer !—God help me, now he's off ;
Reindeer-rider !   Liar :   Hei !
Will you listen !—No, he's striding
O'er the meadow——— !   [*Shrieks.*]   Help .   I'm
    dizzy !

>   Two Old Women, *with sacks on their backs,*
>   *come down the path to the mill.*

FIRST WOMAN.

Christ, who's screaming ?

ÅSE.

>   It is I !

SECOND WOMAN.

Åse !   Well, you are exalted !

ÅSE.

This won't be the end of it ;—
Soon, God help me, I'll be heaven-high

FIRST WOMAN.

Bless your passing !

ÅSE.

>   Fetch a ladder ;
I must be down !   That devil Peer———

SECOND WOMAN.

Peer! Your son?

ÅSE.

Now you can say
You have seen how he behaves.

FIRST WOMAN.

We'll bear witness.

ÅSE.

Only help me;
Straight to Hegstad will I hasten——

SECOND WOMAN.

Is he there?

FIRST WOMAN.

You'll be revenged, then;
Aslak Smith will be there too.

ÅSE.

[*Wringing her hands.*]

Oh, God help me with my boy;
They will kill him ere they're done!

FIRST WOMAN.

Oh, that lot has oft been talked of;
Comfort you: what must be must be!

SECOND WOMAN.

She is utterly demented. [*Calls up the hill.*
Eivind, Anders! Hei! Come here!

A MAN'S VOICE.

What's amiss?

SECOND WOMAN.

Peer Gynt has perched his
Mother on the mill-house roof!

SCENE SECOND.

A hillock, covered with bushes and heather. **The high-**
road runs behind it ; a fence between.

PEER GYNT *comes along a footpath, goes quickly up*
to the fence, stops, and looks out over the distant
prospect.

PEER.

Yonder lies Hegstad. Soon I'll have reached it.
　　　[Puts one leg over the fence ; then hesitates.
Wonder if Ingrid's alone in the house now ?
　　　[Shades his eyes with his hand, and looks out.
No; to the farm guests are swarming like midges.—
H'm, to turn back now perhaps would be wisest.
　　　[Draws back his leg.
Still they must titter behind your back,
And whisper so that it burns right through you.
　　　[Moves a few steps away from the fence, and
　　　begins absently plucking leaves.
Ah, if I'd only a good strong dram now.
Or if I could pass to and fro unseen.—
Or were I unknown.— Something proper and strong
Were the best thing of all, for the laughter don't
　　bite then.
　　　[Looks around suddenly as though afraid ;
　　　then hides among the bushes. Some
　　　WEDDING-GUESTS [1] *pass by, going down-*
　　　wards towards the farm.

A MAN.

[In conversation as they pass.]

His father was drunken, his mother is weak.

---

[1] "Sendingsfolk," literally, "folks with presents." When the
Norwegian peasants are bidden to a wedding-feast, they bring
with them presents of eatables.

A Woman.

Ay, then it's no wonder the lad's good for nought.
> [*They pass on.   Presently* Peer Gynt
> *comes forward, his face flushed with
> shame.   He peers after them.*

Peer.
[*Softly.*]

Was it me they were talking of?
> [*With a forced shrug.*
> Oh, let them chatter?

After all, they can't sneer the life out of my
    body.
> [*Casts himself down upon the heathery
> slope ; lies for some time flat on his back
> with his hands under his head, gazing up
> into the sky.*

What a strange sort of cloud!   It is just like a
    horse.
There's a man on it too—and a saddle—and
    bridle.—
And after it comes an old crone on a broomstick.
> [*Laughs quietly to himself.*
It is mother.   She's scolding and screaming : You
    beast !
Hei you, Peer Gynt—— [*His eyes gradually close.*
    Ay, now she is frightened.—
Peer Gynt he rides first, and there follow him
    many.—
  His steed it is gold-shod and crested with
    silver.
Himself he has gauntlets and sabre and scabbard.
  His cloak it is long, and its lining is silken.
Full brave is the company riding behind him.
  None of them, though, sits his charger so
    stoutly.

None of them glitters like him in the sunshine.—
   Down by the fence stand the people in clusters,
Lifting their hats, and agape gazing upwards.
      Women are curtseying. All the world knows
         him,
Kaiser Peer Gynt, and his thousands of hench-
   men.
   Sixpenny pieces and glittering shillings
Over the roadway he scatters like pebbles.
   Rich as a lord grows each man in the parish.
High o'er the ocean Peer Gynt goes a-riding.
   Engelland's Prince on the seashore awaits him ;
There too await him all Engelland's maidens.
   Engelland's nobles and Engelland's Kaiser,
See him come riding and rise from their banquet.
      Raising his crown, hear the Kaiser address
         him——

ASLAK THE SMITH.

[*To some other young men, passing along the road.*]
Just look at Peer Gynt there, the drunken
   swine—— !

PEER.

[*Starting half up.*]

What, Kaiser—— !

THE SMITH.

[*Leaning against the fence and grinning.*]
            Up with you, Peer, my lad

PEER.

What the devil ?   The smith !   What do you
   want here ?

THE SMITH.

[*To the others.*]

He hasn't got over the Lundëspree yet.

PEER.

[Jumping up.]

You'd better be off!

THE SMITH.

I am going, yes.
But tell us, where have you dropped from, man?
You've been gone six weeks. Were you troll-
    taken, eh?

PEER.

I have been doing strange deeds, Aslak Smith!

THE SMITH.

[Winking to the others.]

Let us hear them, Peer!

PEER.

They are nought to you.

THE SMITH.

[After a pause.]

You're going to Hegstad?

PEER.

No.

THE SMITH.

Time was
They said that the girl there was fond of you.

PEER.

You grimy crow——!

THE SMITH.

[Falling back a little.]

Keep your temper, Peer
Though Ingrid has jilted you, others are left;—
Think—son of Jon Gynt! Come on to the feast;

You'll find there both lambkins and well-seasoned
    widows——

PEER.

To hell——

THE SMITH.

          You will surely find one that will
have you.—
Good evening! I'll give your respects to the
    bride.—
          [They go off, laughing and whispering.

PEER.

   *[Looks after them a while, then makes a defiant
      motion and turns half round.]*

For my part, may Ingrid of Hegstad go marry
Whoever she pleases.   It's all one to me.
           [Looks down at his clothes.
My breeches are torn.   I am ragged and grim.—
If only I had something new to put on now.
             [Stamps on the ground.
If only I could, with a butcher-grip,
Tear out the scorn from their very vitals!
             [Looks round suddenly.
What was that?   Who was it that tittered behind
    there?
H'm, I certainly thought——   No no, it was no
    one.—
I'll go home to mother.
      *[Begins to go upwards, but stops again and
        listens towards Hegstad.*
          They're playing a dance!
      *[Gazes and listens; moves downwards step
        by step, his eyes glisten; he rubs his
        hands down his thighs.*
How the lasses do swarm!   Six or eight to a man!
Oh, galloping death,—I must join in the frolic!—

But how about mother, perched up on the mill-
      house——

> [*His eyes are drawn downwards again; he
> leaps and laughs.*

Hei, how the Halling[1] flies over the green !
Ay, Guttorm, he can make his fiddle speak out !
It gurgles and booms like a foss[2] o'er a scaur.
And then all that glittering bevy of girls !—
Yes, galloping death, I must join in the frolic !

> [*Leaps over the fence and goes down the
> road.*

SCENE THIRD.

*The farm-place at Hegstad.   In the background, the
dwelling-house.   A* Throng of Guests. *A
lively dance in progress on the green.* The
Fiddler *sits on a table.* The Kitchen-master[3]
is standing in the doorway. Cookmaids *are
going to and fro between the different buildings.
Groups of* Elderly People *sit here and there,
talking.*

A Woman.

[*Joins a group that is seated on some logs of wood.*]
The bride ?   Oh yes, she is crying a bit;
But that, you know, isn't worth heeding.

The Kitchen-master.
[*In another group.*]
Now then, good folk, you must empty the barrel.

A Man.
Thanks to you, friend ; but you fill up too quick.

---

[1] A somewhat violent peasant dance.
[2] Foss (in the North of England "force")—a waterfall.
[3] A sort of master of ceremonies.

A LAD.

[*To the* FIDDLER, *as he flies past, holding a* GIRL *by the hand.*]

To it now, Guttorm, and don't spare the fiddle-
strings !

THE GIRL.

Scrape till it echoes out over the meadows !

OTHER GIRLS.

[*Standing in a ring round a lad who is dancing.*]
That's a rare fling !

A GIRL.

He has legs that can lift him '

THE LAD.
[*Dancing.*]

The roof here is high,₁ and the walls wide asunder !

THE BRIDEGROOM.

[*Comes whimpering up to his* FATHER, *who is standing talking with some other men, and twitches his
jacket.*]

Father, she will not ; she is so proud !

HIS FATHER.

What won't she do ?

THE BRIDEGROOM.
She has locked herself in.

HIS FATHER.

Well, you must manage to find the key.

---

¹ To kick the rafters is considered a great feat in the Halling-
dance. The boy means that, in the open air, his leaps are not
limited even by the rafters.

THE BRIDEGROOM

I don't know how.

HIS FATHER.

You're a nincompoop !
[*Turns away to the others. The* BRIDE-
GROOM *drifts across the yard.*

A LAD.

[*Comes from behind the house.*]
Wait a bit, girls !　Things 'll soon be lively.
Here comes Peer Gynt.

THE SMITH.

[*Who has just come up.*]
　　　　　Who invited him ?

THE KITCHEN-MASTER.

　　　　　　No one.
　　　　[*Goes towards the house.*

THE SMITH

[*To the girls.*]
If he should speak to you, never take notice !

A GIRL.

[*To the others.*]
No, we'll pretend that we don't even see him.

PEER GYNT.

[*Comes in heated and full of animation, stops right
in front of the group, and claps his hands.*]
Which is the liveliest girl of the lot of you?

A GIRL.

[*As he approaches her.*]
I am not.

ANOTHER.
[*Similarly.*]
I am not.

A THIRD.
No ; nor I either.

PEER.
[*To a fourth.*]
You come along, then, for want of a better.

THE GIRL.
Haven't got time.

PEER.
[*To a fifth.*]
Well then, you !

THE GIRL.
[*Going.*]
I'm for home.

PEER.
To-night ? are you utterly out of your senses ? [1]

THE SMITH.
[*After a moment, in a low voice.*]
See, Peer, she's taken a greybeard for partner.

PEER.
[*Turns sharply to an elderly man.*]
Where are the unbespoke girls?

THE MAN.
Find them out.
[*Goes away from him.*

[1] A marriage party among the peasants will often last several days.

PEER GYNT *has suddenly become subdued. He
glances shyly and furtively at the group. All
look at him, but no one speaks. He approaches
other groups. Wherever he goes there is silence ;
when he moves away they look after him and
smile.*

PEER.
[*To himself.*]
Mocking looks; needle-keen whispers[1] and smiles.
They grate like a sawblade under the file !
[*He slinks along close to the fence.* SOLVEIG,
leading little HELGA *by the hand, comes
into the yard, along with her* PARENTS.

A MAN.
[*To another, close to* PEER GYNT.]
Look, here are the new folk.

THE OTHER.
The ones from the west?

THE FIRST MAN.
Ay, the people from Hedal.

THE OTHER.
Ah yes, so they are.
PEER.
[*Places himself in the path of the new-comers, points
to* SOLVEIG, *and asks the* FATHER :]
May I dance with your daughter ?

THE FATHER.
[*Quietly.*]
You may so ; but first
We must go to the farm-house and greet the good
people.   [*They go in.*

_____
[1] Literally, "thoughts."

The Kitchen-master.

[*To* Peer Gynt, *offering him drink.*]

Since you are here, you'd best take a pull at the
　　liquor.

Peer.

[*Looking fixedly after the new-comers.*]

Thanks; I'm for dancing; I am not athirst.

　　　　　[*The* Kitchen-master *goes away from
　　　　　him.* Peer Gynt *gazes towards the
　　　　　house and laughs.*

How fair! Did ever you see the like !

Looked down at her shoes and her snow-white
　　apron—!

And then she held on to her mother's skirt-folds,

And carried a psalm-book wrapped up in a
　　kerchief— !

I must look at that girl.

　　　　　　　　　　　[*Going into the house.*

A Lad.

[*Coming out of the house, with several others.*]

　　　　　　　　Are you off so soon, Peer,

From the dance ?

Peer.

No, no.

The Lad.

　　　　　　Then you're heading amiss !

　　　　　[*Takes hold of his shoulder to turn him
　　　　　round.*

Peer.

Let me pass !

The Lad.

I believe you're afraid of the smith.

PEER.

I afraid !

THE LAD.

You remember what happened at Lundë?
*[They go off, laughing, to the dancing-
green.*

SOLVEIG.

[In the doorway of the house.]
Are you not the lad that was wanting to dance ?

PEER.

Of course it was me ; don't you know me again ?
[Takes her hand.
Come, then !

SOLVEIG.

We mustn't go far, mother said.

PEER.

Mother said ! Mother said ! Were you born
yesterday ? [1]

SOLVEIG.

Now you're laughing—— !

PEER.

Why sure, you are almost a child.
Are you grown up ?

SOLVEIG.

I read with the pastor last spring.[2]

PEER.

Tell me your name, lass, and then we'll talk
easier.

1 Literally, " last year."
2 " To read with the pastor," the preliminary to confirmation,
is currently used as synonymous with " to be confirmed."

SOLVEIG.

My name is Solveig.   And what are you called ?

PEER.

Peer Gynt.

SOLVEIG.
[*Withdrawing her hand.*]
 Oh heaven !

PEER.

Why, what is it now ?

SOLVEIG.

My garter is loose ; I must tie it up tighter.
[*Goes away from him.*

THE BRIDEGROOM.
[*Pulling at his MOTHER's gown.*]
Mother, she will not—— !

HIS MOTHER.

She will not ?   What ?

THE BRIDEGROOM.

She won't, mother——

HIS MOTHER.
What ?

THE BRIDEGROOM.

Unlock the door.

HIS FATHER.
[*Angrily, below his breath.*]
Oh, you're only fit to be tied in a stall

HIS MOTHER.

Don't scold him.   Poor dear, he'll be all right yet.
                                   [*They move away.*

A LAD.

[*Coming with a whole crowd of others from
          the dancing-green.*]

Peer, have some brandy?

PEER.

No.

THE LAD.

Only a drain?

PEER.

[*Looking darkly at him.*]

Got any?

THE LAD.

Well, I won't say but I have.
          [*Pulls out a pocket flask and drinks.*

Ah !   How it stings your throat !—Well?

PEER.

Let me try it.
          [*Drinks.*

ANOTHER LAD.

Now you must try mine as well, you know.

PEER.

No!

THE LAD.

Oh, what nonsense ; now don't be a fool.

Take a pull, Peer !

PEER.
Well then, give me a drop.
[*Drinks again.*

A GIRL.
[*Half aloud.*]
Come, let's be going.

PEER.
Afraid of me, wench?

A THIRD LAD.
Who isn't afraid of you?

A FOURTH.
At Lundë
You showed us clearly what tricks you could play.

PEER.
I can do more than that, when I once get started

THE FIRST LAD.
[*Whispering.*]
Now he's forging ahead!

SEVERAL OTHERS.
[*Forming a circle around him.*]
Tell away!   Tell away!
What can you—— ?

PEER.
To-morrow!

OTHERS.
No, now, to-night!

A GIRL.
Can you conjure, Peer?

PEER.

I can call up the devil!

A MAN.

My grandam could do that before I was born!

PEER,

Liar!   What *I* can do, that no one else can.
I one day conjured him into a nut.
It was worm-bored, you see!

SEVERAL.

[*Laughing.*]

Ay, that's easily guessed!

PEER.

He cursed, and he wept, and he wanted to bribe me
With all sorts of things——

ONE OF THE CROWD.

But he had to go in?

PEER.

Of course.   I stopped up the hole with a peg.
Hei!   If you'd heard him rumbling and grumbling!

A GIRL.

Only think!

PEER.

It was just like a humble-bee buzzing.

THE GIRL.

Have you got him still in the nut?

PEER.

Why, no;
By this time that devil has flown on his way.
The grudge the smith bears me is all his doing

A LAD.

Indeed?

PEER.

I went to the smithy, and begged
That he would crack that same nutshell for me.
He promised he would!—laid it down on his anvil;
But Aslak, you know, is so heavy of hand;—
For ever swinging that great sledge-hammer——

A VOICE FROM THE CROWD.

Did he kill the foul fiend?

PEER.

He laid on like a man.
But the devil showed fight, and tore off in a flame
Through the roof, and shattered the wall asunder.

SEVERAL VOICES.

And the smith—— ?

PEER.

Stood there with his hands all scorched.
And from that day onwards, we've never been
friends.   [*General laughter.*

SOME OF THE CROWD.

That yarn is a good one.

OTHERS.

About his best.

PEER.

Do you think I am making it up?

A Man.

Oh no,
That you're certainly not; for I've heard the most
on't
From my grandfather——

PEER.

Liar !   It happened to me

THE MAN.

Yes, like everything else.

PEER.
[*With a fling.*]
I can ride, I can,
Clean through the air, on the bravest of steeds !
Oh, many's the thing I can do, I tell you !
[*Another roar of laughter.*

ONE OF THE GROUP.

Peer, ride through the air a bit !

MANY.

Do, dear Peer Gynt—— !

PEER.

You may spare you the trouble of begging so hard.
I will ride like a hurricane over you all !
Every man in the parish shall fall at my feet !

AN ELDERLY MAN.

Now he is clean off his head.

ANOTHER.

The dolt !

A Third.

Braggart !

A Fourth.
Liar !

Peer.
[*Threatening them.*]
Ay, wait till you see !

A Man.
[*Half drunk.*]
Ay, wait ; you'll soon get your jacket dusted !

Others.

Your back beaten tender ! Your eyes painted
blue !
[*The crowd disperses, the elder men angry,
the younger laughing and jeering.*

The Bridegroom.
[*Close to* Peer Gynt.]
Peer, is it true you can ride through the air ?

Peer.
[*Shortly.*]

It's all true, Mads ! You must know I'm a rare
one !

The Bridegroom.
Then have you got the Invisible Cloak too ?

Peer.

The Invisible Hat, do you mean ? Yes, I have.
[*Turns away from him.* Solveig *crosses
the yard, leading little* Helga.

PEER.

[Goes towards them ; his face lights up.]
Solveig !   Oh, it is well you have come ⸐
                [Takes hold of her wrist.
Now will I swing you round fast and fine !

SOLVEIG.

Loose me ⸍

PEER.

Wherefore ?

SOLVEIG.

            You are so wild.

PEER.

The reindeer is wild, too, when summer is dawning.
Come then, lass ; do not be wayward now !

SOLVEIG.

[Withdrawing her arm.]

Dare not.

PEER.

Wherefore ?

SOLVEIG.

            No, you've been drinking.
            [Moves off with HELGA.

PEER.

Oh, if I had but my knife-blade driven
Clean through the heart of them,—one and all !

THE BRIDEGROOM.

[Nudging him with his elbow.]
Peer, can't you help me to get at the bride ?

PEER.

[*Absently.*]

The bride ?   Where is she ?

THE BRIDEGROOM.

In the store-house.

PEER.

Ah.

THE BRIDEGROOM.

Oh, dear Peer Gynt, you must try at least !

PEER.

No, you must get on without my help.

> [*A thought strikes him ; he says softly but
> sharply.*

Ingrid !   The store-house !

> [*Goes up to* SOLVEIG.

Have you thought better on't?

> [SOLVEIG *tries to go ; he blocks her path.*

You're ashamed to, because I've the look of a tramp.

SOLVEIG.

[*Hastily.*]

No, that you haven't ; that's not true at all !

PEER.

Yes !   And I've taken a drop as well ;
But that was to spite you, because you had hurt me.
Come then !

SOLVEIG.

Even if I wished to, I daren't.

PEER.

Who are you frightened of ?

SOLVEIG.

Father, most.

PEER.

Father?   Ay, ay; he is one of the quiet ones!
One of the godly, eh ?—Answer, come !

SOLVEIG.

What shall I say ?

PEER.

Is your father a psalm-singer? [1]
And you and your mother as well, no doubt?
Come, will you speak ?

SOLVEIG.

Let me go in peace.

PEER.

No !   [*In a low but sharp and threatening tone.*
I can turn myself into a troll !
I'll come to your bedside at midnight to-night.
If you should hear some one hissing and spitting,
You mustn't imagine it's only the cat.
It's me, lass !   I'll drain out your blood in a cup,
And your little sister, I'll eat her up ;
Ay, you must know I'm a were-wolf at night ;—
I'll bite you all over the loins and the back——
          [*Suddenly changes his tone, and entreats, as
              if in dread :*
Dance with me, lass !

SOLVEIG.

[*Looking darkly at him.*]
You were ugly then.
          [*Goes into the house*
          Literally, " A reader."

THE BRIDEGROOM.
[*Comes sidling up again.*]
I'll give you an ox if you'll help me !

PEER.
Then come !
[*They go out behind the house. At the same
moment a crowd of men come forward from
the dancing green; most of them are drunk.
Noise and hubbub.* SOLVEIG, HELGA, *and
their* PARENTS *appear among a number of
elderly people in the doorway.*

THE KITCHEN-MASTER.
[*To the* SMITH, *who is the foremost of the crowd.*
Keep peace now !

THE SMITH.
[*Pulling off his jacket.*]
No, we must fight it out here.[1]
Peer Gynt or I must be taught a lesson.[2]

SOME VOICES.
Ay, let them fight for it !

OTHERS.
No, only wrangle !

THE SMITH.
Fists must decide ; for the case is past words.

SOLVEIG'S FATHER.
Control yourself, man !

[1] Literally, " Here shall judgment be called for."
[2] Literally, " Must be bent to the hillside," made to bite the
dust—but not in the sense of being killed.

HELGA.
Will they beat him, mother?

A LAD.
Let us rather taunt him with all his lies

ANOTHER.
Kick him out of the company.

A THIRD.
Spit in his eyes .

A FOURTH.
[*To the* SMITH.]
You're not backing out, smith?

THE SMITH.
[*Flinging away his jacket.*]
The jade shall be slaughtered!

SOLVEIG'S MOTHER.
[*To* SOLVEIG.]
There, you can see how that windbag is thought
of.

ÅSE.
[*Coming up with a stick in her hand.*]
Is that son of mine here?   Now he's in for a
drubbing !
Oh ! how heartily I will dang him !

THE SMITH.
[*Rolling up his shirt-sleeves.*]
That switch is too light for a carcase like his.

SOME OF THE CROWD.

The smith will dang him!

OTHERS.

Bang him!

THE SMITH.

[*Spits on his hands and nods to* ÅSE.]

Hang him!

ÅSE.

What? Hang my Peer? Ay, just try if you
dare;—
Åse and I,[1] we have teeth and claws!—
Where is he? [*Calls across the yard.*] Peer!

THE BRIDEGROOM.

[*Comes running up.*]

Oh, God's death on the cross!
Come father, come mother, and—— !

HIS FATHER.

What is the matter?

THE BRIDEGROOM.

Just fancy, Peer Gynt—— !

ÅSE.

[*Screams.*]

Have you taken his life?

THE BRIDEGROOM.

No, but Peer Gynt—— ! Look, there on the hillside—— !

THE CROWD.

With the bride

' A peasant idiom.

ÅSE.
[*Lets her stick sink.*]
Oh, the beast!

THE SMITH.
[*As if thunderstruck.*]
Where the slope rises sheerest
He's clambering upwards, by God, like a goat!

THE BRIDEGROOM.
[*Crying.*]
He's shouldered her, mother, as I might a pig!

ÅSE.
[*Shaking her fist up at him.*]
Would God you might fall, and——!
[*Screams out in terror.*
Take care of your footing!

THE HEGSTAD FARMER.
[*Comes in, bare-headed and white with rage.*]
I'll have his life for this bride-rape yet!

ÅSE.
Oh no, God punish me if I let you!

ACT SECOND

SCENE FIRST.

*A narrow path, high up in the mountains. Early
    morning.*
PEER GYNT *comes hastily and sullenly along the path.*
    INGRID, *still wearing some of her bridal orna-
    ments, is trying to hold him back.*

PEER.

Get you from me '

INGRID.
[*Weeping.*]
After this, Peer?

Whither?

PEER.
Where you will for me.

INGRID.
[*Wringing her hands.*]
Oh, what falsehood!

PEER.
Useless railing
Each alone must go his way.

INGRID.
Sin—and sin again unites us!

PEER.

Devil take all recollections !
Devil take the tribe of women—
All but one—— !

INGRID.

Who is that one, pray ?

PEER.

'Tis not you.

INGRID.

Who is it then ?

PEER.

Go !   Go thither whence you came !
Off !   To your father !

INGRID.

Dearest, sweetest——

PEER.

Peace !

INGRID.

You cannot mean it, surely,
What you're saying ?

PEER.

Can and do.

INGRID.

First to lure—and then forsake me !

PEER.

And what terms have you to offer ?

INGRID.

Hegstad Farm, and more besides.

PEER.

Is your psalm-book in your kerchief?
Where's the gold-mane on your shoulders?
Do you glance adown your apron?
Do you hold your mother's skirt-fold?
Speak!

INGRID.

No, but——

PEER.

Went you to the Pastor[1]
This last spring-tide?

INGRID.

No, but Peer——

PEER.

Is there shyness in your glances?
When I beg, can you deny?

INGRID.

Heaven! I think his wits are going.

PEER.

Does your presence sanctify?[2]
Speak!

INGRID.

No, but——

PEER.

What's all the rest then?
[Going.

[1] See note on page 35.
[2] "Blir der Helg når en dig ser?" literally, "Does it become
a holy-day (or holy-tide) when one sees you?"

INGRID.

[*Blocking his way.*]

Know you it will cost your neck
Should you fail me?

PEER.

What do I care?

INGRID.

You may win both wealth and honour
If you take me——

PEER.

Can't afford.

INGRID.

[*Bursting into tears.*]

Oh, you lured me——!

PEER.

You were willing.

INGRID.

I was desperate!

PEER.

Frantic I.

INGRID.

[*Threatening.*]

Dearly shall you pay for this!

PEER.

Dearest payment cheap I'll reckon.

INGRID.

Is your purpose set?

PEER.
Like flint.

INGRID.
Good! we'll see, then, who's the winner !
[*Goes downwards.*

PEER.
[*Stands silent a moment, then cries :*]
Devil take all recollections !
Devil take the tribe of women !

INGRID.
[*Turning her head, and calling mockingly upwards :*]
All but one !

PEER.
Yes, all but one.
[*They go their several ways.*

SCENE SECOND.

Near a mountain tarn ; the ground is soft and marshy
round about. A storm is gathering.
ÅSE *enters, calling and gazing around her despairingly,*
in every direction. SOLVEIG *has difficulty in*
keeping up with her. SOLVEIG'S FATHER *and*
MOTHER, *with* HELGA, *are some way behind.*

ÅSE.
[*Tossing about her arms, and tearing her hair.*]
All things are against me with wrathful might !
Heaven, and the waters, and the grisly mountains !
Fog-scuds from heaven roll down to bewilder
    him

The treacherous waters are lurking to murder
    him !
The mountains would crush him with landslip and
    rift !—
And the people too !   They're out after his life !
God knows they shan't have it !   I can't bear to
    lose him !
Oh, the oaf ! to think that the fiend should tempt
    him !

> [*Turning to* SOLVEIG.

Now isn't it clean unbelievable this ?
He, that did nought but romance and tell lies ;—
He, whose sole strength was the strength of his
    jaw ;
He, that did never a stroke of true work ;—
He——— !   Oh, a body could both cry and laugh !—
    Oh, we clung closely in sorrow and need.
Ay, you must know that my husband, he drank,
Loafed round the parish to roister and prate,
Wasted and trampled our gear under foot.
And meanwhile at home there sat Peerkin
    and I—
The best we could do was to try to forget ;
For ever I've found it so hard to bear up.
It's a terrible thing to look fate in the eyes ;
And of course one is glad to be quit of one's
    cares,
And try all one can to hold thinking aloof.
Some take to brandy, and others to lies ;
And we—why we took to fairy-tales
Of princes and trolls and of all sorts of beasts ;
And of bride-rapes as well.   Ah, but who could
    have dreamt
That those devil's yarns would have stuck in his
    head ?

> [*In a fresh access of terror.*

Hu !   What a scream !   It's the nixie or droug ! [1]
Peer !   Peer!—Up there on that hillock——!
> [*She runs to the top of a little rise, and looks
> out over the tarn.*   SOLVEIG'S FATHER
> *and* MOTHER *come up.*

ÅSE.

Not a sign to be seen !

THE FATHER.
> [*Quietly.*]
>> It is worst for him !

ÅSE.
> [*Weeping.*]
Oh, my Peer !   Oh, my own lost lamb !

THE FATHER.
> [*Nods mildly.*]
You may well say lost.

ÅSE.
>> Oh no, don't talk like that !
He is so clever.   There's no one like him.

THE FATHER.
You foolish woman !

ÅSE.
>> Oh ay ; oh ay ;
Foolish I am, but the boy's all right !

THE FATHER.
> [*Still softly and with mild eyes.*]
His heart is hardened, his soul is lost.

---

[1] A malevolent water-monster.

Åse.

[*In terror.*]

No, no, he can't be so hard, our Lord!

The Father.

Do you think he can sigh for his debt of sin?

Åse.

[*Eagerly.*]

No, but he can ride through the air on a buck,
    though!

The Mother.

Christ, are you mad?

The Father.

Why, what do you mean?

Åse.

Never a deed is too great for him.
You shall see, if only he lives so long——

The Father.

Best if you saw him on the gallows hanging.

Åse.

[*Shrieks.*]

Oh, cross of Christ!

The Father.

In the hangman's hands,
It may be his heart would be turned to re-
    pentance.

Åse.

[*Bewildered.*]

Oh, you'll soon talk me out of my senses!
We must find him!

THE FATHER.
To rescue his soul.

ÅSE.
And his body !
If he's stuck in the swamp, we must drag him
out ;
If he's taken by trolls, we must ring the bells for
him.

THE FATHER.
H'm !—Here's a sheep-path——

ÅSE.
The Lord will repay you
Your guidance and help !

THE FATHER.
It's a Christian's duty.

ÅSE.
Then the others, fie ! they are heathens all ;
There was never a one that would go with us——

THE FATHER.
They knew him too well.

ÅSE.
He was too good for them !
[*Wrings her hands.*
And to think—and to think that his life is at stake!

THE FATHER.
Here are tracks of a man.

ÅSE.
Then it's here we must search !

THE FATHER.

We'll scatter around on this side of our sæter.[1]

[*He and his wife go on ahead.*

SOLVEIG.

[*To* Åse.]

Say on; tell me more.

ÅSE.

[*Drying her eyes.*]

Of my son, you mean?

SOLVEIG.

Yes;—

Tell everything!

ÅSE.

[*Smiles and tosses her head.*]

Everything?—Soon you'd be tired!

SOLVEIG.

Sooner by far will you tire of the telling
Than I of the hearing.

SCENE THIRD.

*Low, treeless heights, close under the mountain moor-
    lands; peaks in the distance. The shadows are
    long; it is late in the day.*
PEER GYNT *comes running at full speed, and stops
    short on the hillside.*

PEER.

The parish is all at my heels in a pack!

[1] *Sæter*—a châlet, or small mountain farm, where the cattle
are sent to pasture in the summer months.

Every man of them armed or with gun or with club.
Foremost I hear the old Hegstad-churl howling.—
Now it's noised far and wide that Peer Gynt is
    abroad !
It is different, this, from a bout with a smith !
This is life ! Every limb grows as strong as a
    bear's.
> [*Strikes out with his arms and leaps in the
>   air.*

To crush, overturn, stem the rush of the foss !¹
To strike ! Wrench the fir-tree right up by the
    root !
This is life ! This both hardens and lifts one high !
To hell then with all of the savourless lies !

THREE SÆTER GIRLS.²

[Rush across the hillside, screaming and singing.]
Trond of the Valfjeld !³   Bård and Kårë !
Troll-pack !   To-night would you sleep in our
    arms ?

PEER.

To whom do you call ?

THE GIRLS.

> To the trolls ! to the trolls '

FIRST GIRL.

Trond, come with kindness !

SECOND GIRL.

> Bård, come with force !

THIRD GIRL.

The cots in the sæter are all standing empty

---

¹ See note, p. 29.   ² See Appendix.
³ Pronounce *Vaal-fyeld.*

FIRST GIRL.

Force is kindness!

SECOND GIRL.

　　　　　And kindness is force!

THIRD GIRL.

If lads are awanting, one plays with the trolls.

PEER.

Why, where are the lads, then?

ALL THREE.

[*With a horse-laugh.*]

　　　　　They cannot come hither

FIRST GIRL.

Mine called me his sweetheart and called me his
　　darling.
Now he has married a grey-headed widow.

SECOND GIRL.

Mine met a gipsy-wench north on the upland.
Now they are tramping the country together.

THIRD GIRL.

Mine put an end to our bastard brat.
Now his head's grinning aloft on a stake.

ALL THREE.

Trond of the Valfjeld! Bård and Kårë!
Troll-pack! To-night would you sleep in our arms?

PEER.

[*Stands, with a sudden leap, in the midst of them.*]
I'm a three-headed troll, and the boy for three
　　girls!

THE GIRLS.

Are you such a lad, eh?

PEER.

You shall judge for yourselves!

FIRST GIRL.

To the hut! To the hut!

SECOND GIRL.

We have mead!

PEER.

Let it flow!

THIRD GIRL.

No cot shall stand empty this Saturday night!

SECOND GIRL.
[*Kissing him.*]

He sparkles and glisters like white-heated iron.

THIRD GIRL
[*Doing likewise.*]

Like a baby's eyes from the blackest tarn.

PEER.
[*Dancing in the midst of them.*]

Heavy of heart and wanton of mind.
The eyes full of laughter, the throat of tears!

THE GIRLS.
[*Making mocking gestures towards the mountain-tops,
      screaming and singing.*]

Trond of the Valfjeld! Bård and Kårë!
Troll-pack!—To-night who shall sleep in our arms?
            [*They dance away over the heights, with
            PEER GYNT in their midst.*

SCENE FOURTH.

Among the Rondë mountains. Sunset. Shining snow-
peaks all around.
PEER GYNT *enters, dizzy and bewildered.*

PEER.

Tower over tower arises!
Hei, what a glittering gate!
Stand! Will you stand! It's drifting
Further and further away!
High on the vane the wind-cock
Arches his wings for flight;—
Blue spread the rifts and bluer,
Locked is the fell and barred.—
    What are those trunks and tree-roots,
That grow from the ridge's clefts?
They are warriors heron-footed!
Now they, too, are fading away.
    A shimmering like rainbow-streamers
Goes shooting through eyes and brain.
What is it, that far-off chiming?
What's weighing my eyebrows down?
Hu, how my forehead's throbbing—
A tightening red-hot ring——!
I cannot think who the devil
Has bound it around my head!

[*Sink down*

    Flight o'er the Edge of Gendin—
Stuff and accursed lies!
Up o'er the steepest hill-wall
With the bride,—and a whole day drunk;
Hunted by hawks and falcons,
Threatened by trolls and such,

Sporting with crazy wenches :—
Lies and accursed stuff !

                    [Gazes long upwards.

   Yonder sail two brown eagles.
Southward the wild geese fly.
And here I must splash and stumble
In quagmire and filth knee-deep !

                        [Springs up.

   I'll fly too !   I will wash myself clean in
The bath of the keenest winds !
I'll fly high !   I will plunge myself fair in
The glorious christening-font !
I will soar far over the sæter ;
I will ride myself pure of soul ;
I will forth o'er the salt sea waters,
And high over Engelland's prince !
Ay, gaze as ye may, young maidens ;
My ride is for none of you ;
You're wasting your time in waiting— !
Yet maybe I'll swoop down, too.—
   What has come of the two brown eagles— ?
They've vanished, the devil knows where !—
   There's the peak of a gable rising ;
It's soaring on every hand ;
It's growing from out the ruins ;—
See, the gateway is standing wide !
Ha-ha, yonder house, I know it ;
It's grandfather's new-built farm !
Gone are the clouts from the windows ;
The crazy old fence is gone.
The lights gleam from every casement ;
There's a feast in the hall to-night.
   There, that was the provost clinking
The back of his knife on his glass ;—
There's the captain flinging his bottle,
And shivering the mirror to bits.—

Let them waste ; let it all be squandered !
Peace, mother ; what need we care !
'Tis the rich Jon Gynt gives the banquet ;
Hurrah for the race of Gynt !
What's all this bustle and hubbub ?
Why do they shout and bawl ?
The captain is calling the son in ;—
Oh, the provost would drink my health.
In then, Peer Gynt, to the judgment ;
It rings forth in song and shout :
Peer Gynt, thou art come of great things,
And great things shall come of thee !

> [*Leaps forward, but runs his head against a rock, falls, and remains stretched on the ground.*

SCENE FIFTH.

A hillside, wooded with great soughing trees.   Stars are gleaming through the leaves ; birds are singing in the tree-tops.

A GREEN-CLAD WOMAN *is crossing the hillside ;* PEER GYNT *follows her, with all sorts of lover-like antics.*

THE GREEN-CLAD ONE.

[*Stops and turns round.*]

Is it true ?

PEER.

[*Drawing his finger across his throat.*]

As true as my name is Peer ;—
As true as that you are a lovely woman !
Will you have me ?   You'll see what a fine man
    I'll be ;

You shall neither tread the loom nor turn the
     spindle.
You shall eat all you want, till you're ready to burst.
I never will drag you about by the hair——

THE GREEN-CLAD ONE.

Nor beat me !

PEER.

No, can you think I would !
We kings' sons never beat women and such.

THE GREEN-CLAD ONE.

You're a king's son

PEER.

Yes.

THE G EEN-CLAD ONE.

I'm the Dovrë-King's daughter.

PEER.

Are you !   See there, now, how well that fits in !

THE GREEN-CLAD ONE.

Deep in the Rondë has father his palace.

PEER.

My mother's is bigger, or much I'm mistaken.

THE GREEN-CLAD ONE.

Do you know my father ?   His name is King Brosë.[1]

PEER.

Do you know my mother ?   Her name is Queen Åsë.

THE GREEN-CLAD ONE.

When my father is angry the mountains are riven.

[1] Pronounce Broasë.

PEER.

They reel when my mother by chance falls
　a-scolding.

THE GREEN-CLAD ONE.

My father can kick e'en the loftiest roof-tree.[1]

PEER.

My mother can ride through the rapidest river.

THE GREEN-CLAD ONE.

Have you other garments besides those rags?

PEER.

Ho, you should just see my Sunday clothes!

THE GREEN-CLAD ONE.

My week-day gown is of gold and silk.

PEER.

It looks to me liker tow and straws.

THE GREEN-CLAD ONE.

Ay, there is one thing you must remember :—
This is the Rondë-folk's use and wont:
All our possessions have two-fold form.
When shall you come to my father's hall,
It well may chance that you're on the point
Of thinking you stand in a dismal moraine.

PEER.

Well now, with us its precisely the same.
Our gold will seem to you litter and trash!
And you'll think, mayhap, every glittering pane
Is nought but a bunch of old stockings and clouts.

---

[1] Kicking the rafters is a much-admired exploit in peasant
dancing.　See note, page 30.

THE GREEN-CLAD ONE.
Black t seems white, and ugly seems fair.

PEER.
Big it seems little, and dirty seems clean.

THE GREEN-CLAD ONE.
[*Falling on his neck.*]
Ay, Peer, now I see that we fit, you and I!

PEER.
Like the leg and the trouser, the hair and the comb.

THE GREEN-CLAD ONE.
[*Calls away over the hillside.*]
Bridal-steed! Bridal-steed! Come, bridal-steed mine!

> [*A gigantic pig comes running in with a rope's end for a bridle and an old sack for a saddle.* PEER GYNT *vaults on its back, and seats the* GREEN-CLAD ONE *in front of him.*]

PEER.
Hark-away! Through the Rondë-gate gallop we in!
Gee-up, gee-up, my courser fine!

THE GREEN-CLAD ONE.
[*Tenderly.*]
Ah, but lately I wandered and moped and pined—
One never can tell what may happen to one!

PEER.
[*Thrashing the pig and trotting off.*]
You may know the great by their riding-gear!

SCENE SIXTH.

*The Royal Hall of the King of the Dovrë-Trolls. A
great assembly of* TROLL-COURTIERS, GNOMES,
and BROWNIES. THE OLD MAN OF THE DOVRË
*sits on the throne, crowned, and with his sceptre
in his hand. His* CHILDREN *and* NEAREST
RELATIONS *are ranged on both sides.* PEER
GYNT *stands before him. Violent commotion in
the hall.*

THE TROLL-COURTIERS.

Slay him ! a Christian-man's son has deluded
The Dovrë-King's loveliest maid !

A TROLL-IMP.

May ı hack him on the fingers ?

ANOTHER.
                      May I tug him by the hair ?

A TROLL-MAIDEN.

Hu, hei, let me bite him in the haunches !

A TROLL-WITCH.
[With a ladle.]
Shall he be boiled into broth and bree ?

ANOTHER TROLL-WITCH.
[With a chopper.]
Shall he roast on a spit or be browned in a
    stewpan ?

THE OLD MAN OF THE DOVRË.

Ice to your blood, friends !
          [Beckons his counsellors closer around him.

                              Don't let us talk big.
We've been drifting astern in these latter years ;
We can't tell what's going to stand or to fall,
And there's no sense in turning recruits away.
Besides the lad's body has scarce a blemish,
And he's strongly-built too, if I see aright.
It's true, he has only a single head ;
But my daughter, too, has no more than one.
Three-headed trolls are gone clean out of fashion ;
One hardly sees even a two-header now,
And even those heads are but so so ones.
                        [*To* PEER GYNT.]
It's my daughter, then, you demand of me ?

                              PEER,
Your daughter and the realm to her dowry, yes.

                          THE OLD MAN.
You shall have the half while I'm still alive,
And the other half when I come to die.

                              PEER.
I'm content with that.

                          THE OLD MAN.
                              Ay, but stop, my lad ;—
You also have some undertakings to give.
If you break even one, the whole pact's at an end,
And you'll never get away from here living.
First of all you must swear that you'll never give
      heed
To aught that lies outside the Rondë-hills' bounds;
Day you must shun, and deeds, and each sunlit
      spot.
                              PEER.
Only call me king, and that's easy to keep.

THE OLD MAN.

And next—now for putting your wits to the test.
                    [*Draws himself up in his seat*

THE OLDEST TROLL-COURTIER.
[*To* PEER GYNT.]

Let us see if you have a wisdom-tooth
That can crack the Dovrë-King's riddle-nut!

THE OLD MAN.

What difference is there 'twixt trolls and men?

PEER.

No difference at all, as it seems to me.
Big trolls would roast you and small trolls would
    claw you ;—
With us it were likewise, if only they dared.

THE OLD MAN.

True enough ; in that and in more we're alike.
Yet morning is morning, and even is even,
And there is a difference all the same.—
Now let me tell you wherein it lies :
Out yonder, under the shining vault,
Among men the saying goes : Man, be thyself!"
At home here with us, 'mid the tribe of the
    trolls,
The saying goes : " Troll, to thyself be—enough !"

THE TROLL-COURTIER
[*To* PEER GYNT.]

Can you fathom the depth ?

PEER.

                    It strikes me as misty.

The Old Man.

My son, that " Enough," that most potent and
    sundering
Word, must be graven upon your escutcheon.

Peer.

[Scratching his head.]

Well, but——

The Old Man.

    It must, if you here would be master !

Peer.

Oh well, let it pass ; after all, it's no worse——

The Old Man.

And next you must learn to appreciate
Our homely, everyday way of life.
    [He beckons ; two Trolls *with pigs'-heads,*
    white night-caps, and so forth, bring in
    food and drink.
The cow gives cakes and the bullock mead ;
Ask not if its taste be sour or sweet ;
The main matter is, and you mustn't forget it,
It's all of it home-brewed.

Peer.

[Pushing the things away from him.]

The devil fly off with your home-brewed drinks
I'll never get used to the ways of this land.

The Old Man.

The bowl's given in, and it's fashioned of gold.
Whoso own the gold bowl, him my daughter holds
    dear.

PEER.

[*Pondering.*]

It is written : Thou shalt bridle the natural man ;—
And I daresay the drink may in time seem less
    sour.
So be it !   [*Complies.*

THE OLD MAN.

            Ay, that was sagaciously said.
You spit ?

PEER.

        One must trust to the force of habit.

THE OLD MAN.

And next you must throw off your Christian-man's
    garb ;
For this you must know to our Dovrë's renown :
Here all things are mountain-made, nought's from
    the dale,
Except the silk bow at the end of your tail.

PEER.

[*Indignant.*]

I haven't a tail !

THE OLD MAN.

            Then of course you must get one.
See my Sunday-tail, Chamberlain, fastened to him.

PEER.

I'll be hanged if you do !   Would you make me a
    fool ?

THE OLD MAN.

None comes courting my child with no tail at
    his rear.

PEER.

Make a beast of a man!

THE OLD MAN.

Nay, my son, you mistake;
I make you a mannerly wooer, no more.
A bright orange bow we'll allow you to wear,
And that passes here for the highest of honours.

PEER.
[*Reflectively.*]

It's true, as the saying goes: Man's but a mote.
And it's wisest to follow the fashion a bit.
Tie away!

THE OLD MAN.

You're a tractable fellow, I see.

THE COURTIER.

Just try with what grace you can waggle and
   whisk it!

PEER.
[*Peevishly.*]

Ha, would you force me to go still further?
Do you ask me to give up my Christian faith?

THE OLD MAN.

No, that you are welcome to keep in peace.
Doctrine goes free; upon that there's no duty;
It's the outward cut one must tell a troll by.
If we're only at one in our manners and dress,
You may hold as your faith what to us is a horror.

PEER.

Why, in spite of your many conditions, you are
A more reasonable chap than one might have
   expected.

THE OLD MAN.

We troll-folk, my son, are less black than we're
    painted ;[1]
That's another distinction between you and us.—
But the serious part of the meeting is over ;
Now let us gladden our ears and our eyes.
Music-maid, forth ! Set the Dovrë-harp sounding !
Dancing-maid, forth ! Tread the Dovrë-hall's
    floor !   [*Music and a dance.*

THE COURTIER.

How like you it ?

PEER.

Like it ?   H'm——

THE OLD MAN.

             Speak without fear !
What see you ?

PEER.

      Why something unspeakably grim :[2]
A bell-cow with her hoof on a gut-harp strumming.
A sow in socklets a-trip to the tune.

THE COURTIERS.

Eat him !

THE OLD MAN.

His sense is but human, remember !

TROLL-MAIDENS.

Hu, tear away both his ears and his eyes '

---

[1] Literally, " Better than our reputation."
[2] " Ustyggelig stygt."   " Ustyggelig " seems to be what Mr.
Lewis Carroll calls a portmanteau word, compounded of
" usigelig " = unspeakable, and " styg " = ugly. The words
might be rendered " beyond grimness grim."

THE GREEN-CLAD ONE.
[*Weeping.*]
Hu-hu! And this we must hear and put up with,
When I and my sister make music and dance.

PEER.
Oho, was it you? Well, a joke at the feast,
You must know, is never unkindly meant.

THE GREEN-CLAD ONE.
Can you swear it was so?

PEER.
           Both the dance and the music
Were utterly charming, the cat claw me else.

THE OLD MAN.
This same human nature's a singular thing;
It sticks to people so strangely long.
If it gets a gash in the fight with us,
It heals up at once, though a scar may remain.
My son-in-law, now, is as pliant as any;
He's willingly thrown off his Christian-man's
     garb,
He's willingly drunk from our chalice of mead,
He's willingly fastened the tail to his back,—
So willing, in short, did we find him in all things,
I thought to myself the old Adam, for certain,
Had for good and all been kicked out of doors;
But lo! in two shakes he's atop again!
Ay ay, my son, we must treat you, I see,
To cure this pestilent human nature.

PEER.
What will you do?

THE OLD MAN.

                In your left eye, first,
I'll scratch you a bit, till you see awry;
But all that you see will seem fine and brave.
And then I'll just cut your right window-pane
    out——

PEER.

Are you drunk?

THE OLD MAN.

[*Lays a number of sharp instruments on the table.*]
                See, here are the glazier's tools.
Blinkers you'll wear, like a raging bull.
Then you'll recognise that your bride is lovely,—
And ne'er will your vision be troubled, as now,
With bell-cows harping and sows that dance

PEER.

This is madman's talk!

THE OLDEST COURTIER.

                It's the Dovrë-King speaking;
'Tis he that is wise, and 'tis you that are crazy!

THE OLD MAN.

Just think how much worry and mortification
You'll thus escape from, year out, year in.
You must remember, your eyes are the fountain
Of the bitter and searing lye of tears.

PEER.

That's true; and it says in our sermon-book:
If thine eye offend thee, then pluck it out.
But tell me, when will my sight heal up
Into human sight?

THE OLD MAN.
>Nevermore, my friend.

PEER.
Indeed !   In that case, I'll take my leave.

THE OLD MAN.
What would you without ?

PEER.
>I would go my way.

THE OLD MAN.
No, stop !   It's easy to slip in here,
But outward the Dovrë-King's gate opens not.

PEER.
You wouldn't detain me by force, I hope ?

THE OLD MAN.
Come now, just listen to reason, Prince Peer !
You have gifts for trolldom.   He acts—does he
>not ?—
Even now in a passably troll-like fashion ?
And you'd fain be a troll ?

PEER.
>Yes, I would, sure enough.
For a bride, and a well-managed kingdom to boot,
I can put up with losing a good many things.
But there is a limit to all things on earth.
The tail I've accepted, it's perfectly true ;
But no doubt I can loose what the Chamberlain
>tied.
My breeches I've dropped ; they were old and
>patched ;
But no doubt I can button them on again.

And lightly enough I can slip my cable
From these your Dovrëfied ways of life.
I am willing to swear that a cow is a maid;
An oath one can always eat up again;—
But to know that one never can free oneself,
That one can't even die like a decent soul;
To live as a hill-troll for all one's days—
To feel that one never can beat a retreat,—
As the book has it, that's what your heart is
    set on;
But that is a thing I can never agree to.

THE OLD MAN.

Now, sure as I live, I shall soon lose my temper;
And then I am not to be trifled with.
You pasty-faced loon! Do you know who I am?
First with my daughter you make too free——

PEER.

There you lie in your throat!

THE OLD MAN.

                    You must marry her

PEER

Do you dare to accuse me—— ?

THE OLD MAN.

                    What? Can you deny
That you lusted for her in heart and eye?

PEER.

[With a snort of contempt.]
No more? Who the deuce cares a straw for that?

THE OLD MAN.

It's ever the same with this humankind.

The spirit you're ready to own with your lips,
But in fact nothing counts that your fists cannot
          handle.
So you really think, then, that lust matters
          nought?
Wait; you shall soon have ocular proof of it——

PEER.

You don't catch me with a bait of lies!

THE GREEN-CLAD ONE.

My Peer, ere the year's out, your child will be born.

PEER.

Open doors ⋅ let me go ⋅

THE OLD MAN.

                    In a he-goat's skin,
You shall have the brat after you.

PEER.
[*Mopping the sweat off his brow.*]
                    Would I could waken!

THE OLD MAN.

Shall we send him to the palace?

PEER.

                    You can send him to the parish!

THE OLD MAN.

Well well, Prince Peer; that's your own look-out.
But one thing's certain, what's done is done;
And your offspring, too, will be sure to grow;
Such mongrels shoot up amazingly fast——

PEER.

Old man, don't act like a headstrong ox !
Hear reason, maiden !   Let's come to terms.
You must know I'm neither a prince nor rich ;—
And whether you measure or whether you weigh
    me,
Be sure you won't gain much by making me yours.
       [THE GREEN-CLAD ONE *is taken ill, and is
        carried out by* TROLL-MAIDS.

THE OLD MAN.

[*Looks at him for a while in high disdain; then says :*]
Dash him to shards on the rock-walls, children !

THE TROLL-IMPS.

Oh dad, mayn't we play owl-and-eagle first :
The wolf-game ! Grey-mouse and glow-eyed cat !

THE OLD MAN.

Yes, but quick. I am worried and sleepy. Good-
    night !   [*He goes.*

PEER.

[*Hunted by the* TROLL-IMPS.]
Let me be, devil's imps !
       [*Tries to escape up the chimney.*

THE IMPS.

       Come brownies !   Come nixies !
Bite him behind !

PEER.

    Ow !
   [*Tries to slip down the cellar trap-door.*

THE IMPS.

       Shut up all the crannies!

THE TROLL-COURTIER.

Now the small-fry are happy !

PEER.

[*Struggling with a little* IMP *that has bit himself
fast to his ear.*]

Let go will you, beast

THE COURTIER.

[*Hitting him across the fingers.*]

Gently, you scamp, with a scion of royalty !

PEER.

A rat-hole——— !   [*Runs to it.*

THE IMPS.

Be quick, Brother Nixie, and block it !

PEER.

The old one was bad, but the youngsters are worse!

THE IMPS.

Slash him !

PEER.

Oh, would I were small as a mouse !
          [*Rushing around.*

THE IMPS.

[*Swarming round him.*]

Close the ring ! Close the ring !

PEER.

[*Weeping.*]

Were I only a louse !
          [*He falls.*

THE IMPS.

Now into his eyes !

PEER.

[*Buried in a heap of* IMPS.]
            Mother, help me, I die
            [*Church bells sound far away.*

THE IMPS.

Bells in the mountain!   The Black-Frock's cows!
        [THE TROLLS *take to flight, amid a confused*
            uproar of yells and shrieks.   The palace
            collapses; everything disappears.

SCENE SEVENTH.

Pitch darkness.
PEER GYNT *is heard beating and slashing about him*
    with a large bough.

PEER.

Answer!   Who are you?

A VOICE IN THE DARKNESS.
            Myself.

PEER.

                        Clear the way!
        THE VOICE.
Go roundabout, Peer!   The hill's roomy enough.

PEER.

[*Tries to force a passage at another place, but strikes*
            against something.]
Who are you?

THE VOICE.
Myself.   Can you say the same?

PEER.

I can say what I will ; and my sword can smite !
Mind yourself!   Hu, hei, now the blow falls
    crushing !
King Saul slew hundreds ; Peer Gynt slew thou-
    sands !   [*Cutting and slashing.*
Who are you ?

THE VOICE.
Myself.

PEER.

                    That stupid reply
You may spare ; it doesn't clear up the matter.
What are you?

THE VOICE.
The great Boyg.[1]

PEER.

                        Ah, indeed !
The riddle was black ; now I'd call it grey.
Clear the way then, Boyg !

THE VOICE.
                Go roundabout, Peer !

PEER.
No, through !   [*Cuts and slashes.*
        There he fell !
    [*Tries to advance, but strikes against some-
        thing.*

            Ho ho, are there more here ?

THE VOICE.
The Boyg, Peer Gynt ! the one only one

[1] See Introduction and Appendix.

It's the Boyg that's unwounded, and the Boyg
    that was hurt,
It's the Boyg that is dead, and the Boyg that's
    alive.

PEER.

[Throws away the branch.]

The weapon is troll-smeared;[1] but I have my fists!
[Fights his way forward.

THE VOICE.

Ay, trust to your fists, lad, trust to your body.
Hee-hee, Peer Gynt, so you'll reach the summit.

PEER.

[Falling back again.]

Forward or back, and it's just as far;—
Out or in, and it's just as strait![2]
He is there!   And there!   And he's round
    the bend!
No sooner I'm out than I'm back in the ring.—
Name who you are!   Let me see you!   What are
    you?

THE VOICE.

The Boyg.

PEER.

[Groping around.]

Not dead, not living; all slimy; misty.
Not so much as a shape!   It's as bad as to
    battle
In a cluster of snarling, half-wakened bears!
[Screams.

Strike back at me, can't you!

---

[1] Rendered harmless by magical anointing.
[2] "Atter og fram, det er lige langt;—
    ud og ind, det er lige trangt!"

THE VOICE.

The Boyg isn't mad

PEER.

Strike!

THE VOICE.

The Boyg strikes not.

PEER.

Fight! You shall!

THE VOICE.

The great Boyg conquers, but does not fight.

PEER.

Were there only a nixie here that could prick me!
Were there only as much as a year-old troll!
Only something to fight with. But here there is
    nothing —
Now he's snoring! Boyg!

THE VOICE.

What's your will?

PEER.

Use force!

THE VOICE.

The great Boyg conquers in all things without it,[1]

PEER.

[*Biting his own arms and hands.*]
Claws and ravening teeth in my flesh!
I must feel the drip of my own warm blood.
    [*A sound is heard like the wing-strokes of
        great birds.*

---

[1] " Med lempe," literally " by gentleness " or " easy-going-
ness." " Quiescence " is somewhere near the idea.

BIRD-CRIES.

Comes he now, Boyg?

THE VOICE.

Ay, step by step.

BIRD-CRIES.

All our sisters far off!   Gather here to the tryst

PEER.

If you'd save me now, lass, you must do it quick!
Gaze not adown so, lowly and bending.—
Your clasp-book!   Hurl it straight into his eyes!

BIRD-CRIES.

He totters!

THE VOICE.

We have him.

BIRD-CRIES.

Sisters!   Make haste

PEER.

Too dear the purchase one pays for life
In such a heart-wasting hour of strife.

[Sinks down.

BIRD-CRIES.

Boyg, there he's fallen!   Seize him!   Seize him!
   *[A sound of bells and of psalm-singing is
      heard far away.*

THE BOYG.

[Shrinks up to nothing, and says in a gasp:]
He was too strong.   There were women behind
   him.

SCENE EIGHTH.

Sunrise. The mountain-side in front of Åse's *sæter.*
The door is shut ; all is silent aud deserted.
Peer Gynt *is lying asleep by the wall of the sæter.*

PEER.
[*Wakens, and looks about him with dull and heavy*
eyes. He spits.]
What wouldn't I give for a pickled herring !
[*Spits again, and at the same moment catches*
sight of Helga, *who appears carrying a*
basket of food.
Ha, child, are you there ?   What is it you want ?

HELGA.
It is Solveig——

PEER.
[*Jumping up.*]
Where is she ?

HELGA.
Behind the sæter.

SOLVEIG.
[*Unseen.*]
If you come nearer, I'll run away !

PEER.
[*Stopping short.*]
Perhaps you're afraid I might take you in my
arms ?

SOLVEIG.

For shame !

PEER.

Do you know where I was last night ?—
Like a horse-fly the Dovrë-King's daughter is after
   me.

SOLVEIG.

Then it was well that the bells were set ringing.

PEER.

Peer Gynt's not the lad they can lure astray.—
What do you say ?

HELGA.

[*Crying.*]
Oh, she's running away !
                              [*Running after her.*

Wait !

PEER.

[*Catches her by the arm.*]
Look here, what I have in my pocket !
A silver button, child !   You shall have it,—
Only speak for me !

HELGA.

Let me be ; let me go !

PEER.

There you have it.

HELGA.

Let go ; there's the basket of food.

PEER.

God pity you if you don't——

HELGA.

Uf, how you scare me!

PEER.

[*Gently; letting her go.*]

No, I only meant: beg her not to forget me!

[HELGA *runs off.*

ACT THIRD.

SCENE FIRST.

Deep in the pine-woods. Grey autumn weather. Snow is falling.
PEER GYNT *stands in his shirt-sleeves, felling timber.*

PEER.

[Hewing at a large fir-tree with twisted branches.]
Oh ay, you are tough, you ancient churl;
But it's all in vain, for you'll soon be down.
                    [Hews at it again.
I see well enough you've a chain-mail shirt,
But I'll hew it through, were it never so stout.—
Ay, ay, you're shaking your twisted arms;
You've reason enough for your spite and rage;
But none the less you must bend the knee——!
                    [Breaks off suddenly.
Lies! 'Tis an old tree and nothing more.
Lies! It was never a steel-clad churl;
It's only a fir-tree with fissured bark.—
It is heavy labour this hewing timber;
But the devil and all when you hew and dream
    too.—
I'll have done with it all—with this dwelling in
    mist,
And, broad-awake, dreaming your senses away.—
You're an outlaw, lad! You are banned to the
    woods.   *[Hews for a while rapidly.*
Ay, an outlaw, ay. You've no mother now

To spread your table and bring your food.
If you'd eat, my lad, you must help yourself,
Fetch your rations raw from the wood and
    stream,
Split your own fir-roots[1] and light your own
    fire,
Bustle around, and arrange and prepare things.
Would you clothe yourself warmly, you must stalk
    your deer;
Would you found you a house, you must quarry
    the stones;
Would you build up its walls, you must fell the
    logs,
And shoulder them all to the building-place.—
        [*His axe sinks down; he gazes straight in
        front of him.*
Brave shall the building be.   Tower and vane
Shall rise from the roof-tree, high and fair.
And then I will carve, for the knob on the gable,
A mermaid, shaped like a fish from the navel.
Brass shall there be on the vane and the door-
    locks.
Glass I must see and get hold of too.
Strangers, passing, shall ask amazed:
What is that glittering far on the hillside?
        [*Laughs angrily.*
Devil's own lies!   There they come again.
You're an outlaw, lad!   [*Hewing vigorously.*
            A bark-thatched hovel
Is shelter enough both in rain and frost.
        [*Looks up at the tree.*
Now he stands wavering.   There; only a kick,
And he topples and measures his length on the
    ground;—

    [1] "Tyri," resinous pine-wood which burns with a bright
blaze.

The thick-swarming undergrowth shudders around
    him !
         [Begins topping the branches from the
         trunk ; suddenly he listens, and stands
         motionless with his axe in the air.
There's some one after me :—Ay, are you that
    sort,
Old Hegstad-churl ; would you play me false ?
         [Crouches behind the tree, and peeps over it.
A lad ! One only. He seems afraid.
He peers all round him. What's that he hides
'Neath his jacket ? A sickle. He stops and looks
    round,—
Now he lays his hand on a fence-rail flat.
What's this now ? Why does he lean like
    that—— ?
Ugh, ugh ! Why, he's chopped his finger off !
A whole finger off !—He bleeds like an ox.—
Now he takes to his heels with his fist in a clout.
                    [Rises.
What a devil of a lad ! An unmendable [1] finger !
Right off ! And with no one compelling him
    to it !
Ho, now I remember ! It's only thus
You can 'scape from having to serve the King.
That's it. They wanted to send him soldiering,
And of course the lad didn't want to go.—
But to chop off——? To sever for good and
    all—— ?
Ay, think of it—wish it done—will it to
    boot,—
But do it——! No, that's past my under-
    standing !
         [Shakes his head a little ; then goes on with
         his work.

---

[1] "Umistelig "—unlosable, indispensable, irreplaceable.

SCENE SECOND.

A room in ÅSE's *house.   Everything in disorder ; boxes*
standing open ; wearing apparel strewn around
A cat is lying on the bed.
ÅSE *and the* COTTAR'S WIFE *are hard at work packing*
things together and putting them straight.

ÅSE.
[*Running to one side.*]
Kari, come here !

KARI.
What now ?

ÅSE.
[*On the other side.*]

Come here——— ?
Where is——— ?   Where shall I find——— ?   Tell
   me where——— ?
What am I seeking ?   I'm out of my wits !
Where is the key of the chest ?

KARI.
In the key-hole.

ÅSE.
What is that rumbling ?

KARI.
The last cart-load
They're driving to Hegstad.

ÅSE.
[*Weeping.*]
How glad I'd be

In the black chest myself to be driven away !
Oh, what must a mortal abide and live through !
God help me in mercy The whole house is
  bare !
What the Hegstad-churl left now the Bailiff [1] has
  taken.
Not even the clothes on my back have they
  spared.
Fie ! Shame on them all that have judged so
  hardly !
                    [*Seats herself on the edge of the bed.*
Both the land and the farm-place are lost to our
  line ;
The old man was hard, but the law was still
  harder ;—
There was no one to help me, and none would
  show mercy ;
Peer was away ; not a soul to give counsel.

KARI.

But here, in this house, you may dwell till you die.

ÅSE.

Ay, the cat and I live on charity.

KARI.

God help you, mother ; your Peer's cost you dear.

ÅSE.

Peer ? Why, you're out of your senses, sure !
Ingrid came home none the worse in the end.
The right thing had been to hold Satan to
  reckoning ;—

---

[1] " Lensmand," the lowest functionary in the Norwegian
official scale—a sort of parish officer.

He was the sinner, ay, he and none other;
The ugly beast tempted my poor boy astray

KARI.

Had I not better send word to the parson?
Mayhap you're worse than you think you are.

ÅSE.

To the parson?   Truly I almost think so.

[*Starts up.*

But, oh God, I can't!   I'm the boy's own mother;
And help him I must; it's no more than my duty;
I must do what I can when the rest forsake him.
They've left him his coat; I must patch it up.
I wish I dared snap up the fur-rug as well!
What's come of the hose?

KARI.

They are there, 'mid that rubbish.

ÅSE.

[*Rummaging about.*]

Why, what have we here?   I declare it's an old
Casting-ladle, Kari!   With this he would play
Button-moulder, would melt, and then shape, and
      then stamp them.
One day—there was company—in the boy came,
And begged of his father a lump of tin.
" Not tin," says Jon, " but King Christian's coin;
Silver; to show you're the son of Jon Gynt."
God pardon him, Jon; he was drunk, you see,
And then he cared neither for tin nor for gold.
Here are the hose.   Oh, they're nothing but
      holes;
They want darning, Kari!

KARI.

Indeed but they do.

ÅSE.

When that is done, I must get to bed;
I feel so broken, and frail, and ill——

[*Joyfully.*

Two woollen-shirts, Kari;—they've passed them
     by !

KARI.

So they have indeed.

ÅSE.

It's a bit of luck.

One of the two you may put aside ;
Or rather, I think we'll e'en take them both ;—
The one he has on is so worn and thin.

KARI.

But oh, Mother Åse, I fear it's a sin.

ÅSE.

Maybe ; but remember the priest holds out
Pardon for this and our other sinnings.

SCENE THIRD.

*In front of a settler's newly-built hut in the forest.
     A reindeer's horns over the door. The snow is
     lying deep around. It is dusk.*
PEER GYNT *is standing outside the door, fastening a
     large wooden bar to it.*

PEER.

[*Laughing between whiles.*]

Bars I must fix me ; bars that can fasten

The door against troll-folk, and men, and women.
Bars I must fix me ; bars that can shut out
All the cantankerous little hobgoblins.—
    They come with the darkness, they knock and
        they rattle :
Open, Peer Gynt, we're as nimble as thoughts are !
    'Neath the bedstead we bustle, we rake in the
        ashes,
Down the chimney we hustle like fiery-eyed
        dragons.
    Hee-hee ! Peer Gynt ; think you staples and
        planks
Can shut out cantankerous hobgoblin-thoughts ?

> [SOLVEIG *comes on snow-shoes over the*
> *heath ; she has a shawl over her head,*
> *and a bundle in her hand.*

SOLVEIG.

God prosper your labour.   You must not reject
    me.
You sent for me hither, and so you must take me.

PEER.

Solveig !   It cannot be——!   Ay, but it is !—
And you're not afraid to come near to me !

SOLVEIG.

One message you sent me by little Helga ;
Others came after in storm and in stillness.
All that your mother told bore me a message,
That brought forth others when dreams sank upon
    me.
Nights full of heaviness, blank, empty days,
Brought me the message that now I must come.
It seemed as though life had been quenched down
    there ;

I could nor laugh nor weep from the depths of my
    heart.
I knew not for sure how you might be minded ;
I knew but for sure what I should do and must do.

PEER.

But your father ?

SOLVEIG.

             In all of God's wide earth
I have none I can call either father or mother.
I have loosed me from all of them.

PEER.

               Solveig, you fair one—
And to come to me ?

SOLVEIG.

             Ay, to you alone ;
You must be all to me, friend and consoler.
                        [*In tears.*
The worst was leaving my little sister ;—
But parting from father was worse, still worse ;
And worst to leave her at whose breast I was
    borne ;—
Oh no, God forgive me, the worst I must call
The sorrow of leaving them all, ay all !

PEER.

And you know the doom that was passed in
    spring ?
It forfeits my farm and my heritage.

SOLVEIG.

Think you for heritage, goods, and gear,
I forsook the paths all my dear ones tread ?

PEER.

And know you the compact ?   Outside the forest
Whoever may meet me may seize me at will.

SOLVEIG.

I ran upon snow-shoes ; I asked my way on ;
They said " Whither go you ? " I answered, " I go
    home."

PEER.

Away, away then with nails and planks !
No need now for bars against hobgoblin-thoughts.
If you dare dwell with the hunter here,
I know the hut will be blessed from ill.
Solveig !   Let me look at you !   Not too near !
Only look at you !   Oh, but you are bright and
    pure !
Let me lift you !   Oh, but you are fine and light !
Let me carry you, Solveig, and I'll never be tired !
I will not soil you.   With outstretched arms
I will hold you far out from me, lovely and warm
    one !
Oh, who would have thought I could draw you to
    me,—
Ah, but I have longed for you, daylong and night-
    long.
Here you may see I've been hewing and build-
    ing ;—
It must down again, dear ; it is ugly and mean——

SOLVEIG.

Be it mean or brave,—here is all to my mind.
One so lightly draws breath in the teeth of the
    wind.
Down below it was airless ; one felt as though
    choked ;

That was partly what drove me in fear from the
    dale.
But here, with the fir-branches soughing o'er-
    head,—
What a stillness and song !—I am here in my home.

PEER.

And know you that surely ?   For all your days ?

SOLVEIG.

The path I have trodden leads back nevermore.

PEER.

You are mine then ! In ! In the room let me see
    you !
Go in ! I must go to fetch fir-roots [1] for fuel.
Warm shall the fire be and bright shall it shine,
You shall sit softly and never be a-cold.
> [*He opens the door ; * SOLVEIG *goes in. He
> stands still for a while, then laughs aloud
> with joy and leaps into the air.*

PEER.

My king's daughter ! Now I have found her and
    won her !
Hei ! Now the palace shall rise, deeply founded !

*He seizes his axe and moves away ; at the same
moment an* OLD-LOOKING WOMAN, *in a tattered
green gown, comes out from the wood ; an* UGLY
BRAT, *with an ale-flagon in his hand, limps after,
holding on to her skirt.*

THE WOMAN.

Good evening, Peer Lightfoot !

[1] See note, p. 92.

PEER.

What is it?   Who's there?

THE WOMAN.

Old friends of yours, Peer Gynt!   My home is
    near by.
We are neighbours.

PEER.

Indeed!   That is more than I know.

THE WOMAN.

Even as your hut was builded, mine built itself
    too.

PEER.

[*Going.*]

I'm in haste——

THE WOMAN.

Yes, that you are always, my lad;
But I'll trudge behind you and catch you at last.

PEER.

You're mistaken, good woman!

THE WOMAN.

I was so before;
I was when you promised such mighty fine things.

PEER.

I promised——?   What devil's own nonsense is
    this?

THE WOMAN.

You've forgotten the night when you drank with
    my sire?
You've forgot——?

PEER.

I've forgot what I never have known.
What's this that you prate of?   When last did we
    meet?

THE WOMAN.

When last we met was when first we met.
            [*To* THE BRAT.]
Give your father a drink; he is thirsty, I'm sure.

PEER.

Father?   You're drunk, woman!   Do you call
    him——-?

THE WOMAN.

I should think you might well know the pig by
    its skin!
Why, where are your eyes?   Can't you see that
    he's lame
In his shank, just as you too are lame in your
    soul?

PEER.

Would you have me believe—— ?

THE WOMAN.

Would you wriggle away—— ?

PEER.

This long-leggëd urchin——!

THE WOMAN.

He's shot up apace.

PEER.

Dare you, you troll-snout, father on me——?

THE WOMAN.

Come now, Peer Gynt, you're as rude as an ox
                                    [*Weeping.*

Is it my fault if no longer I'm fair,
As I was when you lured me on hillside and lea?
Last fall, in my labour, the Fiend held my back,
And so 'twas no wonder I came out a fright.
But if you would see me as fair as before,
You have only to turn yonder girl out of doors,
Drive her clean out of your sight and your
          mind ;—
Do but this, dear my love, and I'll soon lose my
          snout !

PEER.

Begone from me, troll-witch !

THE WOMAN.

                         Ay, see if I do !

PEER.

I'll split your skull open——!

THE WOMAN.

                         Just try if you dare !
Ho-ho, Peer Gynt, I've no fear of blows !
Be sure I'll return every day of the year.
Through the door, set ajar, I'll peep in at you both.
When you're sitting with your girl on the fireside
          bench,—
When you're tender, Peer Gynt,—when you'd pet
          and caress her,—
I'll seat myself by you, and ask for my share.
She there and I—we will take you by turns.
Farewell, dear my lad, you can marry to-morrow

PEER.

You nightmare of hell !

THE WOMAN.

By-the-bye, I forgot!

You must rear your own youngster, you light-
footed scamp!

Little imp, will you go to your father?

THE BRAT.

[*Spits at him.*]

Faugh!

I'll chop you with my hatchet; only wait, only
wait!

THE WOMAN.

[*Kisses* THE BRAT.]

What a head he has got on his shoulders, the
dear!

You'll be dad's living image when once you're a
man!

PEER.

[*Stamping.*]

Oh, would you were as far——!

THE WOMAN.

As we now are near?

PEER.

[*Clenching his hands.*]

And all this——!

THE WOMAN.

For nothing but thoughts and desires!

It is hard on you, Peer!

PEER.

It is worst for another!——

Solveig, my fairest, my purest gold!

THE WOMAN.

Oh ay, 'tis the guiltless must smart, said the devil:
His mother boxed his ears when his father was
    drunk!

> [*She trudges off into the thicket with* THE
> BRAT, *who throws the flagon at* PEER
> GYNT.

PEER.

[After a long silence.]

The Boyg said, " Go roundabout!"—so one must
    here.—
There fell my fine palace, with crash and clatter'
There's a wall around her whom I stood so near,
Of a sudden all's ugly—my joy has grown old.—
Roundabout, lad!   There's no way to be found
Right through all this, from where you stand to her.
Right through?   H'm, surely there should be one.
There's a text on repentance, unless I mistake.
But what?   What is it?   I haven't the book,
I've forgotten it mostly, and here there is none
That can guide me aright in the pathless wood.—
    Repentance?   And maybe 'twould take whole
      years
Ere I fought my way through.   'Twere a meagre
    life, that.
To shatter what's radiant, and lovely, and pure,
And clinch it together in fragments and shards?
You can do it with a fiddle, but not with a bell.
Where you'd have the sward green, you must mind
    not to trample.
    'Twas nought but a lie though, that witch-snout
    business!
Now all that foulness is well out of sight.—
Ay, out of sight maybe, but not out of mind.
Thoughts will sneak stealthily in at my heel.

Ingrid! And the three, they that danced on the
    heights!
Will they too want to join us? With vixenish spite
Will they claim to be folded, like her, to my
    breast,
To be tenderly lifted on outstretched arms?
Roundabout, lad; though my arms were as long
As the root of the fir, or the pine-tree's stem,—
I think even then I should hold her too near
To set her down pure and untarnished again.—
  I must roundabout here, then, as best I may,
And see that it bring me nor gain nor loss.
One must put such things from one, and try to
    forget.—
        [*Goes a few steps towards the hut, but stops
         again.*
  Go in after this? So befouled and disgraced?
Go in with that troll-rabble after me still?
Speak, yet be silent; confess, yet conceal——?
        [*Throws away his axe.*
It's a holy-day evening. For me to keep tryst,
Such as now I am, would be sacrilege.

SOLVEIG.
[*In the doorway.*]
Are you coming?

PEER.
[*Half aloud.*]
Roundabout!

SOLVEIG.
      What?

PEER.
      You must wait.
It is dark, and I've got something heavy to fetch.

SOLVEIG.

Wait; I will help you; the burden we'll share.

PEER.

No, stay where you are! I must bear it alone.

SOLVEIG.

But don't go too far, dear!

PEER.

                Be patient, my girl;
Be my way long or short—you must wait.

SOLVEIG.

[*Nodding to him as he goes.*]
                    Yes, I'll wait
[PEER GYNT *goes down the wood-path.*
SOLVEIG *remains standing in the open
half-door.*]

SCENE FOURTH.

ÅSE's *room. Evening. The room is lighted by a wood
    fire on the open hearth. A cat is lying on a chair
    at the foot of the bed.*
ÅSE *lies in the bed, fumbling about restlessly with her
    hands on the coverlet.*

ÅSE.

Oh, Lord my God, isn't he coming?
    The time drags so drearily on.
I have no one to send with a message;
    And I've much, oh so much, to say.
I haven't a moment to lose now!
    So quickly! Who could have foreseen

Oh me, if I only were certain
  I'd not been too strict with him!

Peer Gynt.
[*Enters.*]

Good evening!
Åse.

          The Lord give you gladness!
You've come then, my boy, my dear!
But how dare you show face in the valley?
  You know your life's forfeit here.

Peer.

Oh, life must e'en go as it may go;
  I felt that I must look in.

Åse.

Ay, now Kari is put to silence,
  And I can depart in peace!

Peer.

Depart?   Why, what are you saying?
  Where is it you think to go?

Åse.

Alas, Peer, the end is nearing;
  I have but a short time left.

Peer.

[*Writhing, and walking towards the back of the room.*]
See there now!   I'm fleeing from trouble;
  I thought at least here I'd be free—— !
Are your hands and your feet a-cold, then?

Åse.

  Ay, Peer; all will soon be o'er.—
When you see that my eyes are glazing,

You must close them carefully.
And then you must see to my coffin;
      And be sure it's a fine one, dear.
Ah no, by-the-bye——

                    PEER.

                        Be quiet !
There's time yet to think of that.

                    ÅSE.

Ay, ay.   [*Looks restlessly round the room.*
            Here you see the little
They've left us !   It's like them, just.

                    PEER.
              [*With a writhe.*]
Again !   [*Harshly.*
            Well, I know it was my fault.
What's the use of reminding me ?

                    ÅSE.

You !   No, that accursed liquor,
      From that all the mischief came !
Dear my boy, you know you'd been drinking;
      And then no one knows what he does;
And besides, you'd been riding the reindeer ;
      No wonder your head was turned !

                    PEER.

Ay, ay ; of that yarn enough now.
      Enough of the whole affair.
All that's heavy we'll let stand over
      Till after—some other day.
                    [*Sits on the edge of the bed.*
Now, mother, we'll chat together ;

   But only of this and that,—
Forget what's awry and crooked,
   And all that is sharp and sore.—
Why see now, the same old pussy
   So she is alive then, still ?

Åse.

She makes such a noise o' nights now ;
   You know what that bodes, my boy :

Peer.
   [*Changing the subject.*]
What news is there here in the parish ?

Åse.
   [*Smiling.*]
   There's somewhere about, they say,
A girl who would fain to the uplands——

Peer.
   [*Hastily.*]
Mads Moen, is he content ?

Åse.

They say that she hears and heeds not
   The old people's prayers and tears.
You ought to look in and see them ;—
   You, Peer, might perhaps bring help——

Peer.
The smith, what's become of him now ?

Åse.
   Don't talk of that filthy smith.

Her name I would rather tell you,
    The name of the girl, you know——

PEER.

Nay, now we will chat together,
    But only of this and that,—
Forget what's awry and crooked,
    And all that is sharp and sore.
Are you thirsty? I'll fetch you water
    Can you stretch you? The bed is short.
Let me see ;—if I don't believe, now,
    It's the bed that I had when a boy !
Do you mind, dear, how oft in the evenings
    You sat at my bedside here,
And spread the fur-coverlet o'er me,
    And sang many a lilt and lay ?

Åse.

Ay, mind you ? And then we played sledges,
    When your father was far abroad.
The coverlet served for sledge-apron,
    And the floor for an ice-bound fiord.

PEER.

Ah, but the best of all, though,—
    Mother, you mind that too ?
The best was the fleet-foot horses——

Åse.

Ay, think you that I've forgot ?—
It was Kari's cat that we borrowed ;
    It sat on the log-scooped chair——

PEER.

To the castle west of the moon, and
    The castle east of the sun,

To Soria-Moria Castle
  The road ran both high and low.
A stick that we found in the closet,
  For a whip-shaft you made it serve.

Åse.

Right proudly I perked on the box-seat——

Peer.

Ay, ay; you threw loose the reins,
And kept turning round as we travelled,
  And asked me if I was cold.
God bless you, ugly old mother,—
  You were ever a kindly soul——!
What's hurting you now?

Åse.

              My back aches,
  Because of the hard, bare boards.

Peer.

Stretch yourself; I'll support you.
  There now, you're lying soft.

Åse.

  [*Uneasily.*]
No, Peer, I'd be moving!

Peer.

              Moving?

Åse.

Ay, moving; 'tis ever my wish.

Peer.

Oh, nonsense!   Spread o'er you the bed-fur.

Let me sit at your bedside here.
There ; now we'll shorten the evening
    With many a lilt and lay.

Åse.

Best bring from the closet the prayer-book :
    I feel so uneasy of soul.

Peer.

In Soria-Moria Castle
    The King and the Prince give a feast.
On the sledge-cushions lie and rest you ;
    I'll drive you there over the heath——

Åse.

But, Peer dear, am I invited ?

Peer.

Ay, that we are, both of us.
> [*He throws a string round the back of the
> chair on which the cat is lying, takes up a
> stick, and seats himself at the foot of the
> bed.*

Gee-up !   Will you stir yourself, Black-boy ?
    Mother, you're not a-cold ?
Ay, ay ; by the pace one knows it,
    When Granë[1] begins to go !

Åse.

Why, Peer, what is it that's ringing—— ?

Peer.

The glittering sledge-bells, dear !

[1] Granë (Grani) was the name of Sigurd Fafnirsbane's horse,
descended from Odin's Sleipnir. Sigurd's Granë was grey :
Peer Gynt calls his " Svarten," Black-boy, or Blackey.—See the
" Volsunga Saga," translated by Morris and Magnussen.
Camelot edition, p. 43.

ÅSE.

Oh, mercy, how hollow it's rumbling.

PEER.

We're just driving over a fiord.

ÅSE.

I'm afraid !   What is that I hear rushing
And sighing so strange and wild ?

PEER.

It's the sough of the pine-trees, mother,
On the heath.   Do you but sit still.

ÅSE.

There's a sparkling and gleaming afar now ;
Whence comes all that blaze of light

PEER.

From the castle's windows and doorways.
Don't you hear, they are dancing ?

ÅSE.

Yes.

PEER.

Outside the door stands St. Peter,
And prays you to enter in.

ÅSE.

Does he greet us ?

PEER.

He does, with honour,
And pours out the sweetest wine.

ÅSE.

Wine !   Has he cakes as well, Peer ?

PEER.

Cakes? Ay, a heaped-up dish.
And the dean's wife[1] is getting ready
Your coffee and your dessert.

ÅSE.

Lord, Lord! shall we two come together?

PEER.

As freely as ever you will.

ÅSE.

Oh, deary, Peer, what a frolic
You're driving me to, poor soul!

PEER.
[Cracking his whip.]
Gee-up; will you stir yourself, Black-boy!

ÅSE.

Peer, dear, you're driving right?

PEER.
[Cracking his whip again.]
Ay, broad is the way.

ÅSE.

This journey,
It makes me so weak and tired.

PEER.

There's the castle rising before us;
The drive will be over soon.

[1] "Salig provstinde," literally "the late Mrs. Provost."

Åse.

I will lie back and close my eyes then,
  And trust me to you, my boy!

Peer.

Come up with you, Granë, my trotter!
  In the castle the throng is great;
They bustle and swarm to the gateway:
  Peer Gynt and his mother are here!
What say you, Master Saint Peter?
  Shall mother not enter in?
You may search a long time, I tell you,
  Ere you find such an honest old soul.
Myself I don't want to speak of;
  I can turn at the castle gate.
If you'll treat me, I'll take it kindly;
  If not, I'll go off just as pleased.
I have made up as many flim-flams
  As the devil at the pulpit desk,
And called my old mother a hen, too,
  Because she would cackle and crow.
But her you shall honour and reverence,
  And make her at home indeed;
There comes not a soul to beat her
  From the parishes nowadays.—
Ho-ho; here comes God the Father!
  Saint Peter! you're in for it now!
                              [*In a deep voice.*
" Have done with these jack-in-office airs, sir;
  Mother Åse shall enter free! "
          [*Laughs loudly, and turns towards his
          mother.*
Ay, didn't I know what would happen?
  Now they dance to another time!   [*Uneasily.*
Why, what makes your eyes so glassy?

Mother!   Have you gone out of your wits—— ?
                    [*Goes to the head of the bed.*
You mustn't lie there and stare so—— !
   Speak, mother; it's I, your boy!
                    [*Feels her forehead and hands cautiously ;
                    then throws the string on the chair, and
                    says softly :*
Ay, ay !—You can rest yourself, Granë ;
   For e'en now the journey's done.
                    [*Closes her eyes, and bends over her.*
For all of your days I thank you,
   For beatings and lullabys !
But see, you must thank me back, now—
                    [*Presses his cheek against her mouth.*
   There ; that was the driver's fare.[1]

THE COTTAR'S WIFE.
[*Entering.*]
What ?   Peer !   Ah, then we are over
   The worse of the sorrow and need !
Dear Lord, but she's sleeping soundly—
   Or can she be—— ?

PEER.
                 Hush ; she is dead.
   [KARI *weeps besides the body ;* PEER GYNT
   *walks up and down the room for some
   time ; at last he stops beside the bed.*

PEER.
See mother buried with honour.
   I must try to fare forth from here.

KARI.
Are you faring afar ?

        Tak for skyds, literally "thanks for the drive."

PEER.
To seaward.

KARI.

So far !

PEER.
Ay, and further still. [*He goes.*

ACT FOURTH

SCENE FIRST.

On the south-west coast of Morocco. A palm-grove.
Under an awning, on ground covered with mat-
ting, a table spread for dinner. Further back in
the grove hammocks are slung. In the offing lies
a steam-yacht, flying the Norwegian and American
colours. A jolly-boat drawn up on the beach. It
is towards sunset.

PEER GYNT, *a handsome middle-aged gentleman, in*
an elegant travelling-dress, with a gold-rimmed
double eyeglass hanging at his waistcoat, is doing
the honours at the head of the table. MR. COTTON,[1]
MONSIEUR BALLON, HERR VON EBERKOPF, *and*
HERR TRUMPETERSTRÅLE,[2] *are seated at the table*
finishing dinner.

PEER GYNT.

Drink, gentlemen ! If man is made
For pleasure, let him take his fill then.
You know 'tis written : Lost is lost,
And gone is gone———. What may I hand you ?

TRUMPETERSTRÅLE.

As host you're princely, Brother Gynt !

---

[1] In the original, "Master Cotton."
[2] A Swede. The name means "trumpet-blast."

PEER.

I share the honour with my cash,
With cook and steward——

MR. COTTON.

　　　　　　Very well;[1]
Let's pledge a toast to all the four!

MONSIEUR BALLON.

Monsieur,[2] you have a *gout*,[2] a *ton*,[2]
That nowadays is seldom met with
Among men living *en garçon*,—[2]
A certain—what's the word——?

VON EBERKOPF.

　　　　　　A dash,
A tinge of free soul-contemplation,
And cosmopolitanisation,[3]
An outlook through the cloudy rifts
By narrow prejudice unhemmed,
A stamp of high illumination,
An *Ur-Natur*,[2] with lore of life,
To crown the trilogy, united.
Nicht wahr, Monsieur, 'twas that you meant?

MONSIEUR BALLON.

Yes, very possible; not quite
So loftily it sounds in French.

VON EBERKOPF.

Ei was![4]　That language is so stiff.——

---

[1] In the original (early editions), "Werry well."
[2] So in original.
[3] This may not be a very lucid or even very precise rendering of *Verdensborgerdomsforpagtning;* but this line, and indeed the whole speech, is pure burlesque; and the exact sense of nonsense is naturally elusive.
[4] So in original.

But the phenomenon's final cause
If we would seek——

PEER.

                    It's found already.
The reason is that I'm unmarried.
Yes, gentlemen, compelety clear
The matter is.   What should a man be?
Himself, is my concise reply.
He should regard himself and his.
But can he, as a sumpter-mule [1]
For others' woe and others' weal?

VON EBERKOPF.

But this same in-and-for-yourself-ness,
I'll answer for't, has cost you strife——

PEER.

Ah yes, indeed; in former days;
But always I came off with honour.
Yet one time I ran very near
To being trapped against my will.
I was a brisk and handsome lad,
And she to whom my heart was given,
She was of royal family——

MONSIEUR BALLON.

Of royal——?

PEER.
[Carelessly.]

            One of those old stocks,
you know the kind——

TRUMPETERSTRÅLE.
[Thumping the table.]

                    Those noble-trolls

---

[1] Literally, "pack-camel."

PEER.

[Shrugging his shoulders.]
Old fossil Highnesses who make it
Their pride to keep plebeian blots
Excluded from their line's escutcheon.

MR. COTTON.
Then nothing came of the affair?

MONSIEUR BALLON.
The family opposed the marriage?

PEER.

Far from it!

MONSIEUR BALLON.
Ah!

PEER.
[With forbearance.]
                    You understand
That certain circumstances made for
Their marrying us without delay.
But truth to tell, the whole affair
Was, first to last, distasteful to me.
I'm finical in certain ways,
And like to stand on my own feet.
And when my father-in-law came out
With delicately veiled demands
That I should change my name and station,
And undergo ennoblement,
With much else that was most distasteful,
Not to say quite inacceptable.—
Why then I gracefully withdrew,
Point-blank declined his ultimatum—
And so renounced my youthful bride.
                    [Drums on the table with a devout air.

Yes, yes ; there is a ruling Fate !
On that we mortals may rely ;
And 'tis a comfortable knowledge.

MONSIEUR BALLON.

And so the matter ended, eh ?

PEER.

Oh no, far otherwise I found it ;
For busy-bodies mixed themselves,
With furious outcries, in the business.
The juniors of the clan were worst ;
With seven of them I fought a duel.
That time I never shall forget,
Though I came through it all in safety.
It cost me blood ; but that same blood
Attests the value of my person,
And points encouragingly towards
The wise control of Fate aforesaid.

VON EBERKOPF.

Your outlook on the course of life
Exalts you to the rank of thinker.
Whilst the mere commonplace empiric
Sees separately the scattered scenes,
And to the last goes groping on,
You in one glance can focus all things.
One norm [1] to all things you apply.
You point each random rule of life,
Till one and all diverge like rays
From one full-orbed philosophy.—
And you have never been to college ?

PEER.

I am, as I've already said,

[1] So in original.

Exclusively a self-taught man.
Methodically naught I've learned ;
But I have thought and speculated,
And done much desultory reading.
I started somewhat late in life,
And then, you know, it's rather hard
To plough ahead through page on page,
And take in all of everything.
I've done my history piecemeal ;
I never have had time for more.
And, as one needs in days of trial
Some certainty to place one's trust in,
I took religion intermittently.
That way it goes more smoothly down.
One should not read to swallow all,
But rather see what one has use for.

MR. COTTON.

Ay, that is practical !

PEER.

[*Lights a cigar.*]
                    Dear friends
Just think of my career in general.
In what case came I to the West ?
A poor young fellow, empty-handed ;
I had to battle sore for bread ;
Trust me, I often found it hard.
But life, my friends, ah, life is dear,
And, as the phrase goes, death is bitter.
Well ! Luck, you see, was kind to me ;
Old Fate, too, was accommodating.
I prospered ; and, by versatility,
I prospered better still and better.
In ten years' time I bore the name
Of Crœsus 'mongst the Charleston shippers.

My fame flew wide from port to port,
And fortune sailed on board my vessels——

MR. COTTON.

What did you trade in?

PEER.

                    I did most
In negro slaves for Carolina,
And idol-images for China.

MONSIEUR BALLON.

Fi donc![1]

TRUMPETERSTRÅLE.
The devil, Uncle Gynt!

PEER.

You think, no doubt, the business hovered
On the outer verge of the allowable?
Myself I felt the same thing keenly.
It struck me even as odious.
But, trust me, when you've once begun,
It's hard to break away again.
At any rate it's no light thing,
In such a vast trade-enterprise,
That keeps whole thousands in employ,
To break off wholly, once for all.
That " once for all " I can't abide,
But own, upon the other side,
That I have always felt respect
For what are known as consequences;
And that to overstep the bounds
Has ever somewhat daunted me.
Besides, I had begun to age.

<hr>

[1] So in original.

Was getting on towards the fifties ;—
My hair was slowly growing grizzled ;
And, though my health was excellent,
Yet painfully the thought beset me :
Who knows how soon the hour may strike,
The jury-verdict be delivered
That parts the sheep and goats asunder ?
    What could I do ?   To stop the trade
With China was impossible.
A plan I hit on—opened straightway
A new trade with the self-same land.
I shipped off idols every spring,
Each autumn sent forth missionaries,
Supplying them with all they needed,
As stockings, Bibles, rum, and rice——

MR. COTTON.

Yes, at a profit ?

PEER.

Why, of course.
It prospered.   Dauntlessly they toiled.
For every idol that was sold
They got a coolie well baptized,
So that the effect was neutralised.
The mission-field lay never fallow,
For still the idol-propaganda
The missionaries held in check.

MR. COTTON.

Well, but the African commodies ?

PEER.

There, too, my ethics won the day.
I saw the traffic was a wrong one
For people of a certain age.

One may drop off before one dreams of it.
And then there were the thousand pitfalls
Laid by the philanthropic camp;
Besides, of course, the hostile cruisers,
And all the wind-and-weather risks.
All this together won the day.
I thought : Now, Peter,[1] reef your sails :
See to it you amend your faults!
So in the South I bought some land,
And kept the last meat-importation,
Which chanced to be a superfine one.
They throve so, grew so fat and sleek,
That 'twas a joy to me, and them too.
Yes, without boasting, I may say
I acted as a father to them,—
And found my profit in so doing.
I built them schools, too, so that virtue
Might uniformly be maintained at
A certain general *niveau*,[1]
And kept strict watch that never its
Thermometer should sink below it.
Now, furthermore, from all this business
I've beat a definite retreat ;—
I've sold the whole plantation, and
It's tale of live-stock, hide and hair.
At parting, too, I served around,
To big and little, gratis grog,[1]
So men and women all got drunk,
And widows got their snuff as well.
So that is why I trust,—provided
The saying is not idle breath :
Whoso does not do ill, does good,—
My former errors are forgotten,
And I, much more than most, can hold
My misdeeds balanced by my virtues.

[1] So in original.

VON EBERKOPF.

[*Clinking glasses with him.*]

How strengthening it is to hear
A principle thus acted out,
Freed from the night of theory,
Unshaken by the outward ferment!

PEER.

[*Who has been drinking freely during the preceding
passages.*]

We Northland men know how to carry
Our battle through!   The key to the art
Of life's affairs is simply this:
To keep one's ear close shut against
The ingress of one dangerous viper.

MR. COTTON.

What sort of viper, pray, dear friend?

PEER.

A little one that slyly wiles you
To tempt the irretrievable.

[*Drinking again.*

The essence of the art of daring,
The art of bravery in act,
Is this: To stand with choice-free foot
Amid the treacherous snares of life,—
To know for sure that other days
Remain beyond the day of battle,—
To know that ever in the rear
A bridge for your retreat stands open
This theory has borne me on,
Has given my whole career its colour;
And this same theory I inherit,
A race-gift, from my childhood's home.

MONSIEUR BALLON.

You are Norwegian ?

PEER.

             Yes, by birth ;
But cosmopolitan in spirit.
For fortune such as I've enjoyed
I have to thank America.
My amply-furnished library
I owe to Germany's later schools.
From France, again, I get my waistcoats,
My manners, and my spice of wit,—
From England an industrious hand,
And keen sense for my own advantage.
The Jew has taught me how to wait.
Some taste for *dolce far niente* [1]
I have received from Italy,—
And one time, in a perilous pass,
To eke the measure of my days,
I had recourse to Swedish steel.

TRUMPETERSTRÅLE.

[*Lifting up his glass.*]

Ay, Swedish steel—— ?

VON EBERKOPF.

             The weapon's wielder
Demands our homage first of all !
     [*They clink glasses and drink with him.
     The wine begins to go to his head.*

MR. COTTON.

All this is very good indeed ;—
But, sir,[1] I'm curious to know
What with your gold you think of doing.

          [1] So in original.

PEER.

[*Smiling.*]

H'm; doing?   Eh?

ALL FOUR.

[*Coming closer.*]
Yes, let us hear!

PEER.

Well, first of all, I want to travel.
You see, that's why I shipped you four,
To keep me company, at Gibraltar.
I needed such a dancing-choir
Of friends around my gold-calf-altar——

VON EBERKOPF.

Most witty!

MR. COTTON.

Well, but no one hoists
His sails for nothing but the sailing.
Beyond all doubt, you have a goal;
And that is—— ?

PEER.

To be Emperor.[1]

ALL FOUR.

What?

PEER.

[*Nodding.*]
Emperor!

THE FOUR.

Where?

---

[1] In the original " kejser." We have elsewhere used the
word "Kaiser," but in this scene, and in Scenes 7 and 8 of this
act, the ordinary English form seemed preferable.

PEER.

O'er all the world.

MONSIEUR BALLON.

But how, friend——?

PEER.

By the might of gold!
That plan is not at all a new one;
It's been the soul of my career.
Even as a boy, I swept in dreams
Far o'er the ocean on a cloud.
I soared with train and golden scabbard,—
And flopped down on all-fours again.
But still my goal, my friends, stood fast.—
There is a text, or else a saying,
Somewhere, I don't remember where,
That if you gained the whole wide world,
But lost yourself, your gain were but
A garland on a cloven skull.
That is the text— or something like it;
And that remark is sober truth.

VON EBERKOPF.

But what then is the Gyntish Self?

PEER.

The world behind my forehead's arch,
In force of which I'm no one else
Than I, no more than God's the Devil.

TRUMPETERSTRÅLE.

I understand now where you're aiming!

MONSIEUR BALLON.

Thinker sublime!

VON EBERKOPF.
Exalted poet !

PEER.
[More and more elevated.]
The Gyntish Self—it is the host
Of wishes, appetites, desires,—
The Gyntish Self, it is the sea
Of fancies, exigencies, claims,
All that, in short, makes my breast heave,
And whereby I, as I, exist.
But as our Lord requires the clay
To constitute him God o' the world,
So I, too, stand in need of gold,
If I as Emperor would figure.

MONSIEUR BALLON.
You have the gold, though ?

PEER.
Not enough.
Ay, maybe for a nine-days' flourish,
As Emperor *à la* [1] Lippe-Detmold.
But I must be myself *en bloc*,[1]
Must be the Gynt of all the planet,
Sir Gynt[1] throughout, from top to bottom !

MONSIEUR BALLON.
[Enraptured.]
Possess the earth's most exquisite beauty '

VON EBERKOPF.
All century-old Johannisberger !

[1] So in original.

TRUMPETERSTRÅLE.

And all the blades of Charles the Twelfth!

MR. COTTON.

But first a profitable opening
For business——

PEER.

That's already found;
Our anchoring here supplied me with it.
To night we set off, northward ho!
The papers I received on board
Have brought me tidings of importance——!

[*Rises with uplifted glass.*

It seems that Fortune ceaselessly
Aids him who has the pluck to seize it——

THE GUESTS.

Well? Tell us——!

PEER.

Greece is in revolt.

ALL FOUR.

[*Springing up.*]

What! Greece——?

PEER.

The Greeks have risen in Hellas.

THE FOUR.

Hurrah!

PEER.

And Turkey's in a fix!

[*Empties his glass.*

MONSIEUR BALLON.

To Hellas! Glory's gate stands open!
I'll help them with the sword of France!

VON EBERKOPF.
And I with war-whoops—from a distance.

MR. COTTON.
And I as well—by taking contracts!

TRUMPETERSTRÅLE.
Lead on! I'll find again in Bender
The world-renownëd spur-strap-buckles! [1]

MONSIEUR BALLON.
[*Falling on* PEER GYNT'S *neck.*]
Forgive me, friend, that I at first
Misjudged you quite!

VON EBERKOFF.
[*Pressing his hands.*]
                    I, stupid hound,
Took you for next door to a scoundrel!

MR COTTON.
Too strong that; only for a fool——

TRUMPETERSTRÅLE.
[*Trying to kiss him.*]
I, Uncle, for a specimen
Of Yankee riff-raff's meanest spawn——!
Forgive me——!

VON EBERKOPF.
            We've been in the dark——

---

[1] An allusion to the spurs with which Charles XII. is said to
have torn the caftan of the Turkish Vizier who announced to
him that the Sultan had concluded a truce with Russia. The
boots and spurs, it would appear, have been preserved, but with
the buckles missing.

PEER.

What stuff is this?

VON EBERKOPF.
          We now see gathered
In glory all the Gyntish host
Of wishes, appetites, and desires——!

MONSIEUR BALLON.
[*Admiringly.*]
So this is being Monsieur [1] Gynt!

VON EBERKOPF.
[*In the same tone.*]
This I call being Gynt with honour!

PEER.

But tell me—— ?

MONSIEUR BALLON.
          Don't you understand?

PEER.

May I be hanged if I begin to!

MONSIEUR BALLON.

What?   Are you not upon your way
To join the Greeks, with ship and money——?

PEER.
[*Contemptuously.*]
No, many thanks!   I side with strength,
And lend my money to the Turks.

MONSIEUR BALLON.

Impossible!
          So in original.

VON EBERKOPF.

Witty, but a jest!

PEER.

[*After a short silence, leaning on a chair and
assuming a dignified mien.*]

Come, gentlemen, I think it best
We part before the last remains
Of friendship melt away like smoke.
Who nothing owns will lightly risk it.
When in the world one scarce commands
The strip of earth one's shadow covers,
One's born to serve as food for powder.
But when a man stands safely landed,
As I do, then his stake is greater.
Go you to Hellas. I will put you
Ashore, and arm you gratis too.
The more you eke the flames of strife,
The better will it serve my purpose.
Strike home for freedom and for right!
Fight! storm! make hell hot for the Turks ;—
And gloriously end your days
Upon the Janissaries lances.—
But I—excuse me——   [*Slaps his pocket.*
                    I have cash,
And am myself, Sir Peter Gynt.[1]
          [*Puts up his sunshade, and goes into the
          grove, where the hammocks are partly
          visible.*]

TRUMPETERSTRÅLE.

The swinish cur!

MONSIEUR BALLON.

No taste for glory——!

[1] So in original.

MR. COTTON.

Oh, glory's neither here nor there;
But think of the enormous profits
We'd reap if Greece should free herself.

MONSIEUR BALLON.

I saw myself a conqueror,
By lovely Grecian maids encircled.

TRUMPETERSTRÅLE.

Grasped in my Swedish hands, I saw
The great, heroic spur-strap-buckles!

VON EBERKOPF.

I my gigantic Fatherland's
Culture saw spread o'er earth and sea——!

MR. COTTON.

The worst's the loss in solid cash.
God dam![1]   I scarce can keep from weeping!
I saw me owner of Olympus.
If to its fame the mountain answers,
There must be veins of copper in it,
That could be opened up again.
And furthermore, that stream Castalia,[2]
Which people talk so much about,
With fall on fall, at lowest reckoning,
Must mean a thousand horse-power good——

TRUMPETERSTRÅLE.

Still I will go!   My Swedish sword
Is worth far more than Yankee gold!

MR. COTTON.

Perhaps; but, jammed into the ranks,

---

[1] So in original.
[2] Mr. Cotton seems to have confounded Olympus with Parnassus.

Amid the press we'd all be drowned ;
And then where would the profit be ?

MONSIEUR BALLON.

Accurst !   So near to fortune's summit,
And now stopped short beside its grave !

MR. COTTON.

[*Shakes his fist towards the yacht.*]

That long black chest holds coffered up
The nabob's golden nigger-sweat—— !

VON EBERKOPF.

A royal notion !   Quick !   Away !
It's all up with his empire now !
Hurrah !

MONSIEUR BALLON.

What would you ?

VON EBERKOPF

Seize the power !

The crew can easily be bought.
On board then.   I annex the yacht !

MR. COTTON.

You—what—— ?

VON EBERKOPF.

I grab the whole concern !
[*Goes down to the jolly-boat.*

MR. COTTON.

Why then self-interest commands me
To grab my share.   [*Goes after him.*

TRUMPETERSTRÅLE.

What scoundrelism !

MONSIEUR BALLON.

A scurvy business—but—*enfin !* [1]

> [*Follows the others.*

TRUMPETERSTRÅLE.

I'll have to follow, I suppose,—
But I protest to all the world——! [2]   [*Follows.*

SCENE SECOND.

*Another part of the coast.   Moonlight with drifting
    clouds.   The yacht is seen far out, under full
    steam.*
PEER GYNT *comes running along the beach; now
    pinching his arms, now gazing out to sea.*

PEER.

A nightmare !—Delusion !—I'll soon be awake !
She's standing to sea !   And at furious speed !—
Mere delusion !   I'm sleeping !   I'm dizzy and
    drunk !   [*Clenches his hands.*
It's not possible I should be going to die !
                [*Tearing his hair.*
A dream !   I'm determined it shall be a dream !
Oh, horror !   It's only too real, worse luck !
My brute-beasts of friends——!   Do but hear
    me, oh Lord !
Since though art so wise and so righteous——!
    Oh judge——!   [*With upstretched arms.*

---

[1] So in original.
[2] An allusion to the attitude of Sweden during the Danish
War of 1863–64, with special reference to the diplomatic notes
of the Minister for Foreign Affairs, Grev Manderström.   He is
also aimed at in the character of Hussein in the last scene of
this act.   See Introduction.

It is *I*, Peter [1] Gynt! Oh, our Lord, give but heed!
Hold thy hand o'er me, Father; or else I must
    perish!
Make them back the machine! Make them lower
    the gig!
Stop the robbers! Make something go wrong
    with the rigging!
Hear me! Let other folks' business lie over!
The world can take care of itself for the time!—
I'm blessed if he hears me! He's deaf as his
    wont is!
Here's a nice thing! A God that is bankrupt of
    help!   [*Beckons upwards.*
Hist; I've abandoned the nigger-plantation!
And missionaries I've exported to Asia!
Surely one good turn should be worth another!
Oh, help me on board—— !

> [*A jet of fire shoots into the air from the
> yacht, followed by thick clouds of smoke ;
> a hollow report is heard.* PEER GYNT
> *utters a shriek, and sinks down on the
> sands. Gradually the smoke clears away ;
> the ship has disappeared.*

PEER.

[*Softly, with a pale face.*]
                That's the sword of wrath!
In a crack to the bottom, every soul, man and
    mouse!
Oh, for ever blest be the lucky chance——
                    [*With emotion.*
A chance? No, no, it was more than a chance.
I was to be rescued and they to perish.
Oh, thanks and praise for that thou hast kept me,

---

[1] So in original.

Hast cared for me, spite of all my sins !—
                    [*Draws a deep breath.*
What a marvellous feeling of safety and peace
It gives one to know oneself specially shielded !
But the desert !   What about food and drink ?
Oh, something I'm sure to find.   He'll see to
    that.
There's no cause for alarm ;—
                    [*Loud and insinuatingly.*
                    He would never allow
A poor little sparrow like me to perish !
Be but lowly of spirit.   And give him time.
Leave it all in the Lord's hands ; and don't be
    cast down.—   [*With a start of terror.*
Can that be a lion that growled in the reeds——?
                    [*His teeth chattering.*
No, it wasn't a lion.   [*Mustering up courage.*
        A lion, forsooth !
Those beasts, they'll take care to keep out of
    the way.
They know it's no joke to fall foul of their betters.
They have instinct to guide them ;—they feel,
    what's a fact,
That it's dangerous playing with elephants.—
    But all the same——.   I must find a tree.
There's a grove of acacias and palms over there ;
If I once can climb up, I'll be sheltered and safe,—
Most of all if I knew but a psalm or two.
                    [*Clambers up.*
Morning and evening are not alike ;
That text has been oft enough weighed and
    pondered.   [*Seats himself comfortably.*
How blissful to feel so uplifted in spirit !
To think nobly is more than to know oneself rich.
Only trust in Him.   He knows well what share
Of the chalice of need I can bear to drain

He takes fatherly thought for my personal weal;—
                [*Casts a glance over the sea, and whispers
                    with a sigh :*
But economical—no, that he isn't !

SCENE THIRD.

*Night.   An encampment of Moroccan troops on the
    edge of the desert.   Watch-fires, with* SOLDIERS
    resting by them.

A SLAVE.
                [*Enters, tearing his hair.*]
Gone is the Emperor's milk-white charger !

ANOTHER SLAVE.
            [*Enters, rending his garments.*]
The Emperor's sacred robes are stolen !

AN OFFICER.
                [*Enters.*]
A hundred stripes upon the foot-soles
For all who fail to catch the robber !
            [*The troopers mount their horses, and gallop
                away in every direction.*

SCENE FOURTH.

Daybreak.   The grove of acacias and palms.
PEER GYNT *in his tree with a broken branch in his
    hand, trying to beat off a swarm of monkeys.*

PEER.
Confound it !   A most disagreeable night.
                        [*Laying about him.*

Are you there again ?   This is most accursëd !
Now they're throwing fruit.   No, it's something
    else.
A loathsome beast is your Barbary ape !
The Scripture says: Thou shalt watch and fight.
But I'm blest if I can ; I am heavy and tired,
                 [Is again attacked ; impatiently :
I must put a stopper upon this nuisance!
I must see and get hold of one of these scamps,
Get him hung and skinned, and then dress
    myself up,
As best I may, in his shaggy hide,
That the others may take me for one of them-
    selves.——
What are we mortals ?   Motes, no more ;
And it's wisest to follow the fashion a bit.——
Again a rabble !   They throng and swarm.
Off with you !   Shoo !   They go on as though
    crazy.
If only I had a false tail to put on now,——
Only something to make me a bit like a beast.——
What now?   There's a pattering over my
    head—— !   *[Looks up.*
It's the grandfather ape,—with his fists full of
    filth—— !
          [Huddles together apprehensively, and keeps
             still for a while.   The ape makes a
             motion ; PEER GYNT *begins coaxing and*
             wheedling him, as he might a dog.
Ay,—are you there, my good old Bus !
He's a good beast, he is !   He will listen to
    reason !
He wouldn't throw ;—I should think not, indeed !
It is me !   Pip-pip !   We are first-rate friends !
Ai-ai !   Don't you hear, I can talk your language ?
Bus and I, we are kinsfolk, you see ;—

Bus shall have sugar to-morrow——! The beast!
The whole cargo on top of me! Ugh, how
    disgusting!—
Or perhaps it was food! 'Twas in taste—inde-
    finable;
And taste's for the most part a matter of habit.
What thinker is it who somewhere says:
You must spit and trust to the force of habit?—
Now here come the small-fry!

                [*Hits and slashes around him.*
                It's really too bad
That man, who by rights is the lord of creation,
Should find himself forced to——! O murder!
    murder!
The old one was bad, but the youngsters are
    worse!

SCENE FIFTH.

*Early morning.   A stony region, with a view out over
    the desert.   On one side a cleft in the hill, and a
    cave.*

A THIEF *and a* RECEIVER *hidden in the cleft, with the
    Emperor's horse and robes.   The horse, richly
    caparisoned, is tied to a stone.   Horsemen are
    seen afar off.*

THE THIEF.

The tongues of the lances
All flickering and flashing,—
See, see!

THE RECEIVER.

Already my head seems
To roll on the sand-plain!
Woe, woe!

THE THIEF.

[Folds his arms over his breast.]

My father he thieved;
So his son must be thieving.

THE RECEIVER.

My father received;
Still his son is receiving.[1]

THE THIEF.

Thy lot shalt thou bear still;
Thyself shalt thou be still.

THE RECEIVER.

[Listening.]

Steps in the brushwood!
Flee, flee! But where?

THE THIEF.

The cavern is deep,
And the Prophet great!

> *[They make off, leaving the booty behind them. The horsemen gradually disappear in the distance.*

PEER GYNT.

[Enters, cutting a reed whistle.]

What a delectable morning-tide!—
The dung-beetle's rolling his ball in the dust;
The snail creeps out of his dwelling-house.
The morning; ay, it has gold in its mouth.—
It's a wonderful power, when you think of it,

---

[1] This is not to be taken as a burlesque instance of the poet's supposed preoccupation with questions of heredity, but simply as an allusion to the fact that, in the East, thieving and receiving are regular and hereditary professions.

That Nature has given to the light of day.
One feels so secure, and so much more cour-
   ageous,—
One would gladly, at need, take a bull by the
   horns.—
What a stillness all round! Ah, the joys of
   Nature,—
Strange enough I should never have prized them
   before.
Why go and imprison oneself in a city,
For no end but just to be bored by the mob.—
Just look how the lizards are whisking about,
Snapping, and thinking of nothing at all.
What innocence ev'n in the life of the beasts!
Each fulfils the Creator's behest unimpeachably,
Preserving its own special stamp undefaced;
Is itself, is itself, both in sport and in strife,
Itself, as it was at his primal: Be!
                          [*Puts on his eye-glasses.*
A toad. In the middle of a sandstone block.
Petrifaction all around him. His head alone
   peering.
There he's sitting and gazing as though through
   a window
At the world, and is—to himself enough.—
                          [*Reflectively.*
Enough? To himself——? Where is it that's
   written?
I've read it, in youth, in some so-called classic.
In the family prayer-book? Or Solomon's Pro-
   verbs?
Alas, I notice that, year by year,
My memory for dates and for places is fading.
                          [*Seats himself in the shade.*
Here's a cool spot to rest and to stretch out one's
   feet.

Why, look, here are ferns growing—edible roots
        [*Eats a little.*
'Twould be fitter food for an animal ;—
But the text says : Bridle the natural man !
Furthermore it is written : The proud shall be
 humbled,
And whoso abaseth himself, exalted. [*Uneasily.*
Exalted ? Yes, that's what will happen with
 me ;—
No other result can so much as be thought of.
Fate will assist me away from this place,
And arrange matters so that I get a fresh start.
This is only a trial ; deliverance will follow,—
If only the Lord let's me keep my health.
   [*Dismisses his misgivings, lights a cigar,*
    stretches himself, and gazes out over the
    desert.
What an enormous, limitless waste !—
Far in the distance an ostrich is striding.—
What can one fancy was really God's
Meaning in all of this voidness and deadness ?
This desert, bereft of all sources of life ;
This burnt-up cinder, that profits no one ;
This patch of the world, that for ever lies fallow ;
This corpse, that never, since earth's creation,
Has brought its Maker so much as thanks,—
Why was it created ? — How spendthrift is
 Nature !—
Is that sea in the east there, that dazzling
 expanse
All gleaming ? It can't be ; 'tis but a mirage.
The sea's to the west ; it lies piled up behind me,
Dammed out from the desert by a sloping ridge.
   [*A thought flashes through his mind.*
Dammed out ? Then I could—— ? The ridge is
 narrow.

Dammed out ?   It wants but a gap, a canal,—
Like a flood of life would the waters rush
In through the channel, and fill the desert ![1]
Soon would the whole of yon red-hot grave
Spread forth, a breezy and rippling sea.
The oases would rise in the midst, like islands ;
Atlas would tower in green cliffs on the north ;
Sailing-ships would, like stray birds on the wing,
Skim to the south, on the caravans' track.
Life-giving breezes would scatter the choking
Vapours, and dew would distil from the clouds.
People would build themselves town on town,
And grass would grow green round the swaying
        palm-trees.
The southland, behind the Sahara's wall,
Would make a new seaboard for civilisation.
Steam would set Timbuctoo's factories spinning ;
Bornu would be colonised apace ;
The naturalist would pass safely through Habes
In his railway-car to the Upper Nile.
In the midst of my sea, on a fat oasis,
I will replant the Norwegian race ;
The Dalesman's blood is next door to royal ;
Arabic crossing will do the rest.
Skirting a bay, on a shelving strand,
I'll build the chief city, Peeropolis.
The world is decrepit !   Now comes the turn
Of Gyntiana, my virgin land !   [*Springs up.*
Had I but capital, soon 'twould be done.—
A gold key to open the gate of the sea !
A crusade against Death ! The close-fisted old churl
Shall open the sack he lies brooding upon.
Men rave about freedom in every land ;—
Like the ass in the ark, I will send forth a cry

---

[1] This proposal was seriously mooted about ten years after
the appearance of *Peer Gynt.*

O'er the world, and will baptize to liberty
The beautiful, thrall-bounden coasts that shall be.
I must on!   To find capital, eastward or west!
My kingdom—well, half of it, say—for a horse!
                    [*The horse in the cleft neighs.*
A horse!   Ay, and robes!—Jewels too,—and a
      sword!   [*Goes closer.*
It can't be!   It is though——!   But how?   I
      have read,
I don't quite know where, that the will can move
      mountains;—
But how about moving a horse as well——?
Pooh!   Here stands the horse, that's a matter of
      fact;—
For the rest, why, *ab esse ad posse*, et cetera.
                [*Puts on the dress and looks down at it.*
Sir Peter—a Turk, too, from top to toe!
Well, one never knows what may happen to one.—
Gee-up, now, Granë, my trusty steed!
                          [*Mounts the horse.*
Gold-slipper stirrups beneath my feet!—
You may know the great by their riding-gear!
                    [*Gallops off into the desert.*

SCENE SIXTH.

The tent of an Arab chief, standing alone on an oasis.
PEER GYNT, *in his eastern dress, resting on cushions.*
      He is drinking coffee, and smoking a long pipe.
      ANITRA, *and a bevy of* GIRLS, *dancing and*
      singing before him.

CHORUS OF GIRLS.

The Prophet is come!
The Prophet, the Lord, the All-Knowing One,

To us, to us is he come,
O'er the sand-ocean riding!
The Prophet, the Lord, the Unerring One,
To us, to us is he come,
O'er the sand-ocean sailing!
  Wake the flute and the drum!
The Prophet, the Prophet is come!

ANITRA.

His courser is white as the milk is
That streams in the rivers of Paradise.
Bend every knee! Bow every head!
His eyes are as bright-gleaming, mild-beaming
    stars.
Yet none earth-born endureth
The rays of those stars in their blinding splendour!
  Through the desert he came.
Gold and pearl-drops sprang forth on his breast.
Where he rode there was light.
Behind him was darkness;
Behind him raged drought and the simoom.
He, the glorious one, came!
Through the desert he came,
Like a mortal apparelled.
Kaaba, Kaaba stands void;—
He himself hath proclaimed it!

THE CHORUS OF GIRLS.

Wake the flute and the drum!
The Prophet, the Prophet is come!
                [*They continue the dance, to soft music.*

PEER.

I have read it in print—and the saying is true—
That no one's a prophet in his native land.—
This position is very much more to my mind

Than my life over there 'mong the Charleston
    merchants.
There was something hollow in the whole affair,
Something foreign at the bottom, something
    dubious behind it;—
I was never at home in their company,
Nor felt myself really one of the guild.
What tempted me into that galley at all ?
To grub and grub in the bins of trade—
As I think it all over, I can't understand it;—
It happened so; that's the whole affair.—
    To be oneself on a basis of gold
Is no better than founding one's house on the
    sand.
For your watch, and your ring, and the rest of your
    trappings,
The good people fawn on you, grovelling to earth ;
They lift their hats to your jewelled breast-pin ;
But your ring and your breast-pin are not your
    Person.—[1]
A prophet; ay, that is a clearer position.
At least one knows on what footing one stands.
If you make a success, it's yourself that receives
The ovation, and not your pounds-sterling and
    shillings.[2]
One is what one is, and no nonsense about it ;
One owes nothing to chance or to accident,
And needs neither licence nor patent to lean on.—
A prophet; ay, that is the thing for me.
And I slipped so utterly unawares into it,—
Just by coming galloping over the desert,
And meeting these children of nature *en route.*
The Prophet had come to them; so much was clear.
It was really not my intent to deceive——;
There's a difference 'twixt lies and oracular answers;

    [1] Or "ego."   [2] In original, " Pundsterling og shilling."

And then I can always withdraw again.
I'm in no way bound; it's a simple matter—;
The whole thing is private, so to speak;
I can go as I came; there's my horse ready saddled;
I am master, in short, of the situation.

ANITRA.

[*Approaching the tent-door.*]

Prophet and Master!

PEER.

What would my slave?

ANITRA.

The sons of the desert await at thy tent-door;
They pray for the light of thy countenance——

PEER.

Stop!

Say in the distance I'd have them assemble;
Say from the distance I hear all their prayers.
Add that I suffer no menfolk in here!
　　Men, my child, are a worthless crew,—
Inveterate rascals you well may call them!
Anitra, you can't think how shamelessly
They have swind—— I mean they have sinned, my
　　child!—[1]
Well, enough now of that; you may dance for me,
　　damsels!
The Prophet would banish the memories that gall
　　him.

THE GIRLS.

[*Dancing.*]

The Prophet is good! The Prophet is grieving
For the ill that the sons of the dust have wrought!

------

[1] In the original, " De har snydt—— hm ; jeg mener syndet,
mit barn ! "

The Prophet is mild ; to his mildness be praises ;
He opens to sinners his Paradise !

PEER.

[*His eyes following* ANITRA *during the dance.*]
Legs as nimble as drumsticks flitting.
She's a dainty morsel indeed, that wench !
It's true she has somewhat extravagant contours,—
Not quite in accord with the norms of beauty.
But what is beauty ?   A mere convention,—
A coin made current by time and place.
And just the extravagant seems most attractive
When one of the normal has drunk one's fill.
In the law-bound one misses all intoxication.
Either plump to excess or excessively lean ;
Either parlously young or portentously old ;—
The medium is mawkish.—
Her feet—they are not altogether clean ;
No more are her arms ; in especial one of them.
But that is at bottom no drawback at all.
I should rather call it a qualification—
Anitra, come listen !

ANITRA.

[*Approaching.*]
Thy handmaiden hears !

PEER.

You are tempting, my daughter ! The Prophet is
touched.
If you don't believe me, then hear the proof ;—
I'll make you a Houri in Paradise !

ANITRA.

Impossible, Lord !

PEER.

What? You think I am jesting?
I'm in sober earnest, as true as I live!

ANITRA.

But I haven't a soul.

PEER.

Then of course you must get one!

ANITRA.

How, Lord?

PEER.

Just leave me alone for that;—
I shall look after your education.
No soul? Why, truly you're not over bright,
As the saying goes. I've observed it with pain.
But pooh! for a soul you can always find room.
Come here! let me measure your brain-pan, child.—
There is room, there is room, I was sure there was.
It's true you never will penetrate
Very deep; to a large soul you'll scarcely attain;—
But never you mind; it won't matter a bit;—
You'll have plenty to carry you through with
    credit——

ANITRA.

The Prophet is gracious——

PEER.

You hesitate? Speak!

ANITRA.

But I'd rather——

PEER.

Say on; don't waste time about it

ANITRA.

I don't care so much about having a soul;—
Give me rather——

PEER.

What, child?

ANITRA.

[*Pointing to his turban.*]
                          That lovely opal!

PEER.

[*Enchanted, handing her the jewel.*]
Anitra! Anitra! true daughter of Eve!
I feel thee magnetic; for I am a man,
And, as a much-esteemed author has phrased it:
" Das Ewig-Weibliche ziehet uns an! " [1]

SCENE SEVENTH.

A moonlight night. The palm-grove outside ANITRA'S
tent.
PEER GYNT *is sitting beneath a tree, with an Arabian
lute in his hands. His beard and hair are clipped;
he looks considerably younger.*

PEER GYNT.
[*Plays and sings.*]
I double-locked my Paradise,
    And took its key with me.
The north-wind bore me seaward ho!
While lovely women all forlorn
    Wept on the ocean strand.

---

[1] In the previous edition we restored the exact wording of
Goethe's line, " zieht uns hinan." We ought to have understood that the point of the speech lay in the misquotation.

Still southward, southward clove my keel
   The salt sea-currents through.
Where palms were swaying proud and fair,
A garland round the ocean-bight,
   I set my ship afire.

I climbed aboard the desert ship,
   A ship on four stout legs.
It foamed beneath the lashing whip;—
Oh, catch me; I'm a flitting bird;—
   I'm twittering on a bough!

Anitra, thou'rt the palm-tree's must;
   That know I now full well!
Ay, even the Angora goat-milk cheese
Is scarcely half such dainty fare,
   Anitra, ah, as thou!

      [He hangs the lute over his shoulder, and
        comes forward.]

Stillness! Is the fair one listening?
Has she heard my little song?
Peeps she from behind the curtain,
Veil and so forth cast aside?—
Hush! A sound as though a cork
From a bottle burst amain!
Now once more! And yet again!
Love-sighs can it be? or songs?—
No, it is distinctly snoring.—
Dulcet strain! Anitra sleepeth!
Nightingale, thy warbling stay!
Every sort of woe betide thee,
If with gurgling trill thou darest—
But, as says the text: Let be!
Nightingale, thou art a singer;
Ah, even such an one am I.
He, like me, ensnares with music
Tender, shrinking little hearts.

Balmy night is made for music ;
Music is our common sphere ;
In the act of singing, we are
We, Peer Gynt and nightingale.
And the maiden's very sleeping
Is my passion's crowning bliss ;—
For the lips protruded o'er the
Beaker yet untasted quite——
But she's coming, I declare !
After all, it's best she should.

ANITRA.

[*From the tent.*]

Master, call'st thou in the night ?

PEER.

Yes indeed, the Prophet calls.
I was wakened by the cat
With a furious hunting-hubbub——

ANITRA.

Ah, not hunting-noises, Master;
It was something much, much worse.

PEER.

What, then, was't ?

ANITRA.

Oh, spare me !

PEER.

                              Speak .

ANITRA.

Oh, I blush to——

PEER.

[*Approaching.*]

                    Was it, mayhap,
That which filled me so completely
When I let you have my opal ?

ANITRA.
[*Horrified.*]

Liken thee, O earth's great treasure,
To a horrible old cat !

PEER.

Child, from passion's standpoint viewed,
May a tom-cat and a prophet
Come to very much the same.

ANITRA.

Master, jest like honey floweth
From thy lips.

PEER.

My little friend,
You, like other maidens, judge
Great men by their outsides only.
I am full of jest at bottom,
Most of all when we're alone.
I am forced by my position
To assume a solemn mask.
Duties of the day constrain me ;
All the reckonings and worry
That I have with one and all,
Make me oft a cross-grained prophet ;
But it's only from the tongue out.—
Fudge, avaunt !   *En tête-à-tête*
I'm Peer—well, the man I am.
Hei, away now with the prophet ;
Me, myself, you have me here !

[*Seats himself under a tree, and draws her
to him.*

Come, Anitra, we will rest us
Underneath the palm's green fan-shade !
I'll lie whispering, you'll lie smiling ;
Afterwards our rôles exchange we ;

Then shall your lips, fresh and balmy,
To my smiling, passion whisper !

ANITRA.

[Lies down at his feet.]
All thy words are sweet as singing,
Though I understand but little.
Master, tell me, can thy daughter
Catch a soul by listening ?

PEER.

Soul, and spirit's light and knowledge,
All in good time you shall have them.
When in east, on rosy streamers
Golden types print : Here is day,—
Then, my child, I'll give you lessons ;
You'll be well brought up, no fear.
But, 'mid night's delicious stillness,
It were stupid if I should,
With a threadbare wisdom's remnants,
Play the part of pedagogue.—
And the soul, moreover, is not,
Looked at properly, the main thing.
It's the heart that really matters.

ANITRA.

Speak, O Master ! When thou speakest,
I see gleams, as though of opals !

PEER.

Wisdom in extremes is folly ;
Coward blossoms into tyrant ;
Truth, when carried to excess,
Ends in wisdom written backwards.
Ay, my daughter, I'm forsworn
As a dog if there are not

Folk with o'erfed souls on earth
Who shall scarce attain to clearness.
Once I met with such a fellow,
Of the flock the very flower;
And even he mistook his goal,
Losing sense in blatant sound.—
See the waste round this oasis.
Were I but to swing my turban,
I could force the ocean-flood
To fill up the whole concern.
But I were a blockhead, truly
Seas and lands to go creating.
Know you what it is to live?

ANITRA.

Teach me!

PEER.

It is to be wafted
Dry-shod down the stream of time,
Wholly, solely as oneself.
Only in full manhood can I
Be the man I am, dear child!
Aged eagle moults his plumage,
Aged fogey lags declining,
Aged dame has ne'er a tooth left,
Aged churl gets withered hands,—
One and all get withered souls.
Youth! Ah Youth! I mean to reign,
As a sultan, whole and fiery,—
Not on Gyntiana's shores,
Under trellised vines and palm-leaves,—
But enthronëd [1] in the freshness
Of a woman's virgin thoughts.—
    See you now, my little maiden,
Why I've graciously bewitched you,—

Literally, " on the basis of."

Why I have your heart selected,
And established, so to speak,
There my being's Caliphate?
All your longings shall be mine.
I'm an autocrat in passion!
You shall live for me alone.
I'll be he who shall enthrall
You like gold and precious stones.
Should we part, then life is over,—
That is, your life, *nota bene!*
Every inch and fibre of you,
Will-less, without yea or nay,
I must know filled full of me.
Midnight beauties of your tresses,
All that's lovely to be named,
Shall, like Babylonian gardens,
Tempt your Sultan to his tryst.

    After all, I don't complain, then,
Of your empty forehead-vault.
With a soul, one's oft absorbed in
Contemplation of oneself.
Listen, while we're on the subject,—
If you like it, faith, you shall
Have a ring about your ankle:—
'Twill be best for both of us.
I will be your soul by proxy;
For the rest—why, *status quo.*   [ANITRA *snores.*
What! She sleeps! Then has it glided
Bootless past her, all I've said?—
No; it marks my influence o'er her
That she floats away in dreams
On my love-talk as it flows.
                    [*Rises, and lays trinkets in her lap.*
Here are jewels! Here are more!
Sleep, Anitra! Dream of Peer——.
Sleep! In sleeping, you the crown have

Placed upon your Emperor's brow !
Victory on his Person's basis
Has Peer Gynt this night achieved.

SCENE EIGHTH

*A caravan route.   The oasis is seen far off in the
    background.*
PEER GYNT *comes galloping across the desert on his
    white horse, with* ANITRA *before him on his
    saddle-bow.*

ANITRA.

Let be, or I'll bite you !

PEER.

You little rogue !

ANITRA.

What would you ?

PEER.

What would I ?   Play hawk and dove !
Run away with you !   Frolic and frisk a bit !

ANITRA.

For shame !   An old prophet like you !

PEER.

Oh, stuff !

The prophet's not old at all, you goose !
Do you think all this is a sign of age ?

ANITRA.

Let me go !   I want to go home !

PEER.

Coquette !

What, home ! To papa-in-law ! That would be
　fine !
We madcap birds that have flown from the cage
Must never come into his sight again.
Besides, my child, in the self-same place
It's wisest never to stay too long ;
For familiarity lessens respect ;—
Most of all when one comes as a prophet or such.
One should show oneself glimpse-wise and pass
　like a dream.
Faith, 'twas time that the visit should come to an
　end.
They're unstable of soul, are these sons of the
　desert ;—
Both incense and prayers dwindled off towards the
　end.

ANITRA.

Yes, but are you a prophet ?

PEER.

Your Emperor I am !
[Tries to kiss her.
Why just see now how coy the wee woodpecker is !

ANITRA.

Give me that ring that you have on your finger.

PEER.

Take, sweet Anitra, the whole of the trash !

ANITRA.

Thy words are as songs ! Oh, how dulcet their
　sound !

PEER.

How blessëd to know oneself loved to this pitch !

I'll dismount !   Like your slave, I will lead your
    palfrey !
       [*Hands her his riding-whip, and dismounts.*
There now, my rosebud, you exquisite flower !
Here I'll go trudging my way through the sand,
Till a sunstroke o'ertakes me and finishes me.
I'm young, Anitra ; bear that in mind !
You mustn't be shocked at my escapades.
Frolics and high-jinks are youth's sole criterion !
And so, if your intellect weren't so dense,
You would see at a glance, oh my fair oleander,—
Your lover is frolicsome—*ergo,* he's young !

ANITRA.

Yes, you are young.   Have you any more rings ?

PEER.

Am I not ?   There, grab !   I can leap like a buck !
Were there vine-leaves around, I would garland
    my brow.
To be sure I am young !   Hei, I'm going to dance !
       [*Dances and sings.*

      I am a blissful game-cock !
      Peck me, my little pullet !
      Hop-sa-sa !   Let me trip it ;—
      I am a blissful game-cock !

ANITRA.

You are sweating, my prophet; I fear you will
    melt ;—
Hand me that heavy bag hung at your belt.

PEER.

Tender solicitude !   Bear the purse ever ;—
Hearts than can love are content without gold !
       [*Dances and sings again.*

Young Peer Gynt is the maddest wag ;—
He knows not what foot he shall stand upon.
   Pooh, says Peer ;—pooh, never mind !
Young Peer Gynt is the maddest wag !

ANITRA.

What joy when the Prophet steps forth in the
   dance !

PEER.

Oh, bother the Prophet !—Suppose we change
   clothes !
Heisa !   Strip off !

ANITRA.

Your caftan were too long,
Your girdle too wide, and your stockings too
   tight——

PEER.

Eh bien ! [1]   [*Kneels down.*
   But vouchsafe me a vehement sorrow ;—
To a heart full of love, it is sweet to suffer !
Listen ; as soon as we're home at my castle——

ANITRA.

In your Paradise ;—have we far to ride ?

PEER.

Oh, a thousand miles or——

ANITRA.

Too far !

PEER.

Oh, listen ;—
You shall have the soul that I promised you
   once——

[1] So in original.

ANITRA.

Oh, thank you; I'll get on without the soul.
But you asked for a sorrow——

PEER.

[*Rising.*]

Ay, curse me, I did!
A keen one, but short,—to last two or three days

ANITRA.

Anitra obeyeth the Prophet!—Farewell!
　　[*Gives him a smart cut across the fingers, and
　　　dashes off, at a tearing gallop, back across
　　　the desert.*

PEER.

[*Stands for a long time thunderstruck.*]
Well now, may I be—— !

SCENE NINTH.

The same place, an hour later.
PEER GYNT *is stripping off his Turkish costume,
　　soberly and thoughtfully, bit by bit. Last of all,
　　he takes his little travelling-cap out of his coat
　　pocket, puts it on, and stands once more in Euro-
　　pean dress.*

PEER.

[*Throwing the turban far away from him.*]
There lies the Turk, then, and here stand I!—
These heathenish doings are no sort of good.
It's lucky 'twas only a matter of clothes,
And not, as the saying goes, bred in the bone.—

What tempted me into that galley at all?
It's best, in the long run, to live as a Christian,
To put away peacock-like ostentation,
To base all one's dealings on law and morality,
To be ever oneself, and to earn at the last a
Speech at one's grave-side, and wreaths on one's
    coffin.   [*Walks a few steps.*
The hussy;—she was on the very verge
Of turning my head clean topsy-turvy.
May I be a troll if I understand
What it was that dazed and bemused me so.
Well; it's well that's done: had the joke been
    carried
But one step on, I'd have looked absurd.—
I have erred;——but at least it's a consolation
That my error was due to the false situation.
It wasn't my personal self that fell.
'Twas in fact this prophetical way of life,
So utterly lacking the salt of activity,
That took its revenge in these qualms of bad taste.
It's a sorry business this prophetising!
One's office compels one to walk in a mist;
In playing the prophet, you throw up the game[1]
The moment you act like a rational being.[2]
In so far I've done what the occasion demanded,
In the mere fact of paying my court to that goose.
But, nevertheless——   [*Bursts out laughing.*
        H'm, to think of it now!
To try to make time stop by jigging and dancing,
And to cope with the current by capering and
    prancing!
To thrum on the lute-strings, to fondle and sigh,
And end, like a rooster,—by getting well plucked'
Such conduct is truly prophetic frenzy.—

    [1] Literally, " you're looed " or " euchred."
    [2] Literally, " behave as though sober and wakeful.

Yes, plucked !—Phew ! I'm plucked clean enough
    indeed.
Well, well, I've a trifle still left in reserve;
I've a little in America, a little in my pocket ;
So I won't be quite driven to beg my bread.—
And at bottom this middle condition is best.
I'm no longer a slave to my coachman and horses;
I haven't to fret about postchaise or baggage;
I am master, in short, of the situation.—
What path should I choose ? Many paths lie
    before me ;
And a wise man is known from a fool by his
    choice.
My business life is a finished chapter ;
My love-sports, too, are a cast-off garment.
I feel no desire to live back like a crab.
" Forward or back, and it's just as far ;
Out or in, and it's just as strait,"—
So I seem to have read in some luminous[1] work.—
I'll try something new, then; ennoble my course ;
Find a goal worth the labour and money it costs.
Shall I write my life without dissimulation,—
A book for guidance and imitation ?
Or, stay——! I have plenty of time at com-
    mand ;—
What if, as a travelling scientist,
I should study past ages and time's voracity ?
Ay, sure enough, that is the thing for me !
Legends I read e'en in childhood's days,
And since then I've kept up that branch of
    learning.—
I will follow the path of the human race !
Like a feather I'll float on the stream of history
Make it all live again, as in a dream,—
See the heroes battling for truth and right,

        [1] Literally, "*spirituel*."

As an onlooker only, in safety ensconced,—
See thinkers perish and martyrs bleed,
See empires founded and vanish away,—
See world-epochs grow from their trifling seeds ;
In short, I will skim off the cream of history.—
I must try to get hold of a volume of Becker,
And travel as far as I can by chronology.—
It's true—my grounding's by no means thorough,
And history's wheels within wheels are decep-
          tive ;—
But pooh ; the wilder the starting-point,
The result will oft be the more original.—
How exalting it is, now, to choose a goal,
And drive straight for it, like flint and steel !
                              [*With quiet emotion.*
To break off all round one, on every side,
The bonds that bind one to home and friends,—
To blow into atoms one's hoarded wealth,—
To bid one's love and its joys good night,—
All simply to find the arcana of truth,—
                    [*Wiping a tear from his eye.*
That is the test of the true man of science !—
I feel myself happy beyond all measure.
Now I have fathomed my destiny's riddle.
Now 'tis but persevering through thick and thin !
It's excusable, sure, if I hold up my head,
And feel my worth, as the man, Peer Gynt,
Also called Human-life's Emperor.—
I will own the sum-total of bygone days ;
I'll nevermore tread in the paths of the living.
The present is not worth so much as a shoe-sole ;
All faithless and marrowless the doings of men ;
Their soul has no wings and their deeds no
          weight ;——   [*Shrugs his shoulders.*
And women,—ah, they are a worthless crew !
                              [*Goes off.*

SCENE TENTH.

*A summer day.   Far up in the North.   A hut in the
    forest.   The door, with a large wooden bar,
    stands open.   Reindeer-horns over it.   A flock of
    goats by the wall of the hut.*

A MIDDLE-AGED WOMAN, *fair-haired and comely,
    sits spinning outside in the sunshine.*

THE WOMAN.

[Glances down the path and sings.]

Maybe both the winter and spring will pass by,
And the next summer too, and the whole of the
    year ;—
But thou wilt come one day, that know I full well;
And I will await thee, as I promised of old.[1]

                    [Calls the goats, spins, and sings again.

God strengthen thee, whereso thou goest in the
    world !
God gladden thee, if at his footstool thou stand !
Here will I await thee till thou comest again ;
And if thou wait up yonder, then there we'll meet,
    my friend !

SCENE ELEVENTH.

In Egypt.   Daybreak.   MEMNON'S STATUE *amid the
    sands.*

PEER GYNT *enters on foot, and looks around him for
    a while.*

PEER GYNT.

Here I might fittingly start on my wanderings.—

                [1] *Sidst*—literally, "when last we met."

So now, for a change, I've become an Egyptian ;
But Egyptian on the basis of the Gyntish I.
To Assyria next I will bend my steps.
To begin right back at the world's creation
Would lead to nought but bewilderment.
I will go round about [1] all the Bible history ;
It's secular traces I'll always be coming on ;
And to look, as the saying goes, into its seams,
Lies entirely outside both my plan and my
     powers.   [*Sits upon a stone.*
Now I will rest me, and patiently wait
Till the statue has sung its habitual dawn-song.
When breakfast is over, I'll climb up the pyramid;
If I've time, I'll look through its interior after-
     wards.
Then I'll go round the head of the Red Sea by
     land ;
Perhaps I may hit on King Potiphar's grave.——
Next I'll turn Asiatic.   In Babylon I'll seek for
The far-renowned harlots and hanging gardens,——
That's to say, the chief traces of civilisation.
Then at one bound to the ramparts of Troy.
From Troy there's a fareway by sea direct
Across to the glorious ancient Athens ;——
There on the spot will I, stone by stone,
Survey the Pass that Leonidas guarded.
I will get up the works of the better philosophers,
Find the prison where Socrates suffered, a
     martyr—— ;
Oh no, by-the-bye—there's a war there at pre-
     sent—— !
Well, my studies in Hellas must e'en be postponed.
                              [*Looks at his watch.*
It's really too bad, such an age as it takes
For the sun to rise.   I am pressed for time.

     [1] "Gå udenom," the phrase used by the Boyg, Act ii. sc. 7.

Well then, from Troy—it was there I left off——
                              [*Rises and listens.*
What is that strange sort of murmur that's rush-
    ing—— ?   [*Sunrise.*

MEMNON'S STATUE.

[*Sings.*]

From the demigod's ashes there soar, youth-
        renewing,
              Birds ever singing.
              Zeus the Omniscient
              Shaped them contending.
              Owls of wisdom,
My birds, where do they slumber ?
Thou must die if thou rede not
              The song's enigma !

PEER.

How strange now,—I really fancied there came
From the statue a sound.   Music, this, of the
    Past.
I heard   the stone-accents   now rising, now
    sinking.—
I will register it, for the learned to ponder.
                    [*Notes in his pocket-book*
" The statue did sing.   I heard the sound plainly,
But didn't quite follow the text of the song.
The whole thing, of course, was hallucination.—
Nothing else of importance observed to-day."
                        [*Proceeds on his way.*

SCENE TWELFTH.

Near the village of Gizeh. The great SPHINX *carved
    out of the rock. In the distance the spires and
    minarets of Cairo.*
PEER GYNT *enters ; he examines the* SPHINX *atten-
    tively, now through his eyeglass, now through his
    hollowed hand.*

PEER GYNT.

Now, where in the world have I met before
Something half forgotten that's like this hob-
        goblin ?
For met it I have, in the north or the south.
Was it a person ?   And, if so, who ?
That Memnon, it afterwards crossed my mind,
Was like the Old Man of the Dovrë, so called,
Just as he sat there, stiff and stark,
Planted on end on the stumps of pillars.—
But this most curious mongrel here,
This changeling, a lion and woman in one,—
Does he come to me, too, from a fairy-tale,
Or from a remembrance of something real ?
From a fairy-tale ?   Ho, I remember the fellow !
Why, of course it's the Boyg, that I smote on the
        skull,—
That is, I dreamt it,—I lay in fever.—
                                    [*Going closer.*
The self-same eyes, and the self-same lips ;—
Not quite so lumpish ; a little more cunning ;
But the same, for the rest, in all essentials.—
Ay, so that's it, Boyg ; so you're like a lion
When one sees you from behind and meets you in
        the day-time !
Are you still good at riddling ?   Come, let us try.

Now we shall see if you answer as last time!
            [*Calls out towards the* SPHINX.
Hei, Boyg, who are you?

                    A VOICE.
            [*Behind the* SPHINX.]
                    Ach, Sphinx, wer bist du?

                PEER.
What! Echo answers in German! How strange!

                THE VOICE.
Wer bist du?

                    PEER.
            It speaks it quite fluently too!
That observation is new, and my own.
                    [*Notes in his book.*
" Echo in German.   Dialect, Berlin."
        [BEGRIFFENFELDT *comes out from behind*
            the SPHINX.

            BEGRIFFENFELDT.
A man

                PEER.
        Oh, then it was he that was chattering.
                    [*Notes again*
" Arrived in the sequel at other results."

            BEGRIFFENFELDT.
        [*With all sorts of restless antics*]
Excuse me, mein Herr[1]——!   Eine Lebens-
        frage—— ![1]
What brings you to this place precisely to-day?

                PEER.
A visit.   I'm greeting a friend of my youth.

                [1] So in original.

BEGRIFFENFELDT.

What ?   The Sphinx——— ?

PEER.
[*Nods.*]
Yes, I knew him in days gone by.

BEGRIFFENFELDT.

Famos ! [1]—And that after such a night !
My temples are hammering as though they would
    burst !
You know him, man !   Answer !   Say on !   Can
    you tell
What he is ?

PEER.
What he is ?   Yes, that's easy enough.
He's himself.

BEGRIFFENFELDT.
[*With a bound.*]
Ha, the riddle of life lightened forth
In a flash to my vision !—It's certain he is
Himself ?

PEER.
Yes, he says so, at any rate.

BEGRIFFENFELDT.

Himself !   Revolution ! thine hour is at hand !
                              [*Takes off his hat.*
Your name, pray, mein Herr ? [1]

PEER.
I was christened Peer Gynt.

[1] So in original.

BEGRIFFENFELDT.

[In rapt admiration.]

Peer Gynt! Allegoric! I might have foreseen it.—
Peer Gynt? That must clearly imply : The Un-
    known,—
The Comer whose coming was augured to me——

PEER.

What, really? And now you are here to meet——?

BEGRIFFENFELDT.

Peer Gynt! Profound! Enigmatic! Incisive!
Each word, as it were, an abysmal lesson!
What are you?

PEER.

[Modestly.]

I've always endeavoured to be
Myself.   For the rest, here's my passport, you see.

BEGRIFFENFELDT.

Again that mysterious word at the bottom.
                    [Seizes him by the wrist.
To Cairo!   The Interpreters' Kaiser is found!

PEER.

Kaiser?

BEGRIFFENFELDT.

Come on!

PEER.

Am I really known——?

BEGRIFFENFELDT.

[Dragging him away.]

The Interpreters' Kaiser—on the basis of Self!

SCENE THIRTEENTH.

In Cairo.   A large courtyard, surrounded by high
     walls and buildings.   Barred windows ; iron
     cages.
THREE KEEPERS *in the courtyard.   A* FOURTH
     comes in.

THE NEWCOMER.

Schafmann, say, where's the director gone ?

A KEEPER

He drove out this morning some time before
     dawn.

THE FIRST.

I think something must have occurred to annoy
     him ;
For last night——

ANOTHER.

          Hush, be quiet ; he's there at the door !
          [BEGRIFFENFELDT *leads* PEER GYNT *in,*
          locks the gate, and puts the key in his
          pocket.

PEER.

[*To himself.*]

Indeed an exceedingly gifted man ;
Almost all that he says is beyond comprehension.
                              [*Looks around.*
So this is the Club of the Savants, eh ?

BEGRIFFENFELDT

Here you will find them, every man jack of
     them :—

The group of Interpreters threescore and ten;[1]
Of late it has grown by a hundred and sixty——
                    [*Shouts to the* KEEPERS.
Mikkel, Schlingelberg, Schafmann, Fuchs,—
Into the cages with you at once *!*

THE KEEPERS.

We!

BEGRIFFENFELDT.

Who else, pray?   Get in, get in!
When the world twirls around, we must twirl with
    it too.   [*Forces them into a cage.*
He's arrived this morning, the mighty Peer;—
The rest you can guess,—I need say no more.
        [*Locks the cage door, and throws the key
        into a well.*

PEER.

But, my dear Herr Doctor and Director, pray——?

BEGRIFFENFELDT.

Neither one nor the other!   I was before——
Herr Peer, are you secret?   I must ease my
    heart——

PEER.

[*With increasing uneasiness.*]

What is it?

BEGRIFFENFELDT.

Promise you will not tremble.

PEER.

I will do my best, but——

---

[1] This is understood to refer to the authors of the Greek
version of the Old Testament, known as the Septuagint.   We
are unable to account for the hundred and sixty recruits to their
company.

BEGRIFFENFELDT.

[*Draws him into a corner, and whispers.*]
                        The Absolute Reason
Departed this life at eleven last night.

PEER.

God help me—— !

BEGRIFFENFELDT.

                    Why, yes, it's extremely deplorable.
And as I'm placed, you see, it is doubly un-
    pleasant ;
For this institution has passed up to now
For what's called a madhouse.

PEER.

                            A madhouse, ha !

BEGRIFFENFELDT.

Not now, understand '

PEER.

[*Softly, pale with fear.*]
                    Now I see what the place is !
And the man is mad ;—and there's none that
    knows it '   [*Tries to steal away.*

BEGRIFFENFELDT.

[*Following him.*]
However, I hope you don't misunderstand me ?
When I said he was dead, I was talking stuff.
He's beside himself.   Started clean out of his
    skin,—
Just like my compatriot Münchausen's fox.

PEER.

Excuse me a moment——

BEGRIFFENFELDT.
[*Holding him back.*]
    I meant like an eel ;—
It was not like a fox. A needle through his eye ;—
And he writhed on the wall——

PEER.
    Where can rescue be found !

BEGRIFFENFELDT.
A snick round his neck, and whip ! out of his skin .

PEER
He's raving · He's utterly out of his wits !

BEGRIFFENFELDT.
Now it's patent, and can't be dissimulated,
That this from-himself-going must have for result
A complete revolution by sea and land.
The persons one hitherto reckoned as mad,
You see, became normal last night at eleven,
Accordant with Reason in its newest phase.
And more, if the matter be rightly regarded,
It's patent that, at the aforementioned hour,
The sane folks, so called, began forthwith to rave.

PEER.
You mentioned the hour, sir ; my time is but
 scant——

BEGRIFFENFELDT.
Your time, did you say ? There you jog my
 remembrance !
    [*Opens a door and calls out.*
Come forth all ! The time that shall be is pro-
 claimed !
Reason is dead and gone ; long live Peer Gynt !

PEER.

Now, my dear good fellow——!
[*The* LUNATICS *come one by one, and at
intervals, into the courtyard.*

BEGRIFFENFELDT.

Good morning! Come forth,
And hail the dawn of emancipation!
Your Kaiser has come to you!

PEER.

Kaiser?

BEGRIFFENFELDT.

Of course!

PEER.

But the honour's so great, so entirely excessive——

BEGRIFFENFELDT.

Oh, do not let any false modesty sway you
At an hour such as this.

PEER.

But at least give me time——
No, indeed, I'm not fit; I'm completely dumb-
founded!

BEGRIFFENFELDT.

A man who has fathomed the Sphinx's meaning
A man who's himself!

PEER.

Ay, but that's just the rub.
It's true that in everything I am myself;
But here the point is, if I follow your meaning,
To be, so to phrase it, outside oneself.

BEGRIFFENFELDT.

Outside ?   No, there you are strangely mistaken!
It's here, sir, that one is oneself with a vengeance;
Oneself, and nothing whatever besides.
We go, full sail, as our very selves.
Each one shuts himself up in the barrel of self,
In the self-fermentation he dives to the bottom,—
With the self-bung he seals it hermetically,
And seasons the staves in the well of self.
No one has tears for the other's woes;
No one has mind for the other's ideas.
We're our very selves, both in thought and tone,
Ourselves to the spring-board's uttermost verge,—
And so, if a Kaiser's to fill the Throne,
It is clear that you are the very man.

PEER.

O would that the devil —— !

BEGRIFFENFELDT.

                    Come, don't be cast down;
Almost all things in nature are new at the first.
"Oneself";—come, here you shall see an example;
I'll choose you at random the first man that
        comes——   [*To a gloomy figure.*
Good-day, Huhu ?   Well, my boy, wandering
        round
For ever with misery's impress upon you ?

HUHU.[1]

Can I help it, when the people,
Race [2] by race, dies untranslated.[3]
                            [*To* PEER GYNT.
You're a stranger; will you listen ?

    See Introduction.   [2] Literally, "generation."
[3] Literally, "uninterpreted."

PEER.

[*Bowing.*]

Oh, by all means !

HUHU.

                Lend your ear then.—
Eastward far, like brow-borne garlands,
Lie the Malabarish seaboards.
Hollanders and Portugueses
Compass all the land with culture.
There, moreover, swarms are dwelling
Of the pure-bred Malabaris.
These have muddled up the language,
They now lord it in the country.—
But in long-departed ages
There the orang-outang was the ruler.
He, the forest's lord and master,
Freely fought and snarled in freedom.
As the hand of nature shaped him,
Just so grinned he, just so gaped he.
He could shriek unreprehended;
He was ruler in his kingdom.—
Ah, but then the foreign yoke came,
Marred the forest-tongue primeval.
Twice two hundred years of darkness[1]
Brooded o'er the race of monkeys ;
And, you know, nights so protracted
Bring a people to a standstill.—
Mute are now the wood-notes primal;
Grunts and growls are heard no longer ;—
If we'd utter our ideas,
It must be by means of language.
What constraint on all and sundry !
Hollanders and Portugueses,

[1] An allusion to the long period of stagnation in the history of Norway under the Danish rule—say, from 1400 to 1800.

Half-caste race and Malabaris,
All alike must suffer by it.—
I have tried to fight the battle
Of our real, primal wood-speech,—
Tried to bring to life its carcass,—
Proved the people's right of shrieking,—
Shrieked myself, and shown the need of
Shrieks in poems for the people.—
Scantly, though, my work is valued.—
Now I think you grasp my sorrow.
Thanks for lending me a hearing;—
Have you counsel, let me hear it !

PEER.
[Softly.]

It is written : Best be howling
With the wolves that are about you.   [*Aloud.*
Friend, if I remember rightly,
There are bushes in Morocco,
Where orang-outangs in plenty
Live with neither bard nor spokesman ;—
Their speech sounded Malabarish ;—
It was classical and pleasing.
Why don't you, like other worthies,
Emigrate to serve your country ?

HUHU.

Thanks for lending me a hearing ;—
I will do as you advise me.
                    [*With a large gesture.*
East ! thou hast disowned thy singer !
West ! thou hast orang-outangs still !   [*Goes.*

BEGRIFFENFELDT.

Well, was he himself ? I should rather think so.
He's filled with his own affairs, simply and solely.

He's himself in all that comes out of him,—
Himself, just because he's beside himself.
Come here!   Now I'll show you another one
Who's no less, since last evening, accordant with
     Reason.
               [*To a* FELLAH, *with a mummy on his back.*
King Apis, how goes it, my mighty lord?

THE FELLAH.
[*Wildly, to* PEER GYNT.]
Am I King Apis?

PEER.
[*Getting behind the* DOCTOR.]
               I'm sorry to say
I'm not quite at home in the situation;
But I certainly gather, to judge by your tone——

THE FELLAH.
Now you too are lying.

BEGRIFFENFELDT.
               Your Highness should state
How the whole matter stands.

THE FELLAH.
               Yes, I'll tell him my tale.
                    [*Turns to* PEER GYNT.
Do you see whom I bear on my shoulders?
His name was King Apis of old.
Now he goes by the title of mummy,
And withal he's completely dead.
   All the pyramids yonder he builded,
And hewed out the mighty Sphinx,
And fought, as the Doctor puts it,
With the Turks, both to rechts and links.

And therefore the whole of Egypt
Exalted him as a god,
And set up his image in temples,
In the outward shape of a bull.—

But *I* am this very King Apis,
I see that as clear as day;
And if you don't understand it,
You shall understand it soon.

King Apis, you see, was out hunting,
And got off his horse awhile,
And withdrew himself unattended
To a part of my ancestor's land.

But the field that King Apis manured
Has nourished me with its corn;
And if further proofs are demanded,
Know, I have invisible horns.

Now, isn't it most accursëd
That no one will own my might !
By birth I am Apis of Egypt,
But a fellah in other men's sight.

Can you tell me what course to follow ?—
Then counsel me honestly.—
The problem is how to make me
Resemble King Apis the Great.

Peer.

Build pyramids then, your highness,
And carve out a greater Sphinx,
And fight, as the Doctor puts it,
With the Turks, both to rechts and links.

The Fellah.

Ay, that is all mighty fine talking !
A fellah ! A hungry louse !
I, who scarcely can keep my hovel
Clear even of rats and mice.

Quick, man,—think of something better,
That'll make me both great and safe,
And further, exactly like to
King Apis that's on my back !

PEER.

What if your highness hanged you,
And then, in the lap of earth,
'Twixt the coffin's natural frontiers,
Kept still and completely dead.

THE FELLAH.

I'll do it !   My life for a halter !
To the gallows with hide and hair !—
At first there will be some difference,
But that time will smooth away.
          [*Goes off and prepares to hang himself.*

BEGRIFFENFELDT.

There's a personality for you, Herr Peer,—
A man of method——

PEER.

          Yes, yes ; I see——;
But he'll really hang himself !   God grant us
     grace !
I'll be ill;—I can scarcely command my thoughts .

BEGRIFFENFELDT.

A state of transition ; it won't last long.

PEER.

Transition ?   To what ?   With your leave—I must
     go——
          BEGRIFFENFELDT.
          [*Holding him.*].

Are you crazy ?

PEER.

Not yet——.   Crazy ?   Heaven forbid !
[*A commotion.   The Minister* HUSSEIN [1]
forces his way through the crowd.

HUSSEIN.

They tell me a Kaiser has come to-day.
[*To* PEER GYNT.

It is you ?

PEER.

[*In desperation.*]
Yes, that is a settled thing !

HUSSEIN.

Good.—Then no doubt there are notes to be
answered ?

PEER.

[*Tearing his hair.*]
Come on !   Right you are, sir ;—the madder the
better !

HUSSEIN.

Will you do me the honour of taking a dip ?
[*Bowing deeply.*

I am a pen.

PEER.

[*Bowing still deeper.*]
Why then I am quite clearly
A rubbishy piece of imperial parchment.

HUSSEIN.

My story, my lord, is concisely this :
They take me for a pounce-box,[2] and I am a pen.

---

[1] See note, p. 140.
[2] The pounce-box (for strewing " pounce " or sand on undried
ink) had not yet been quite superseded by blotting-paper.

PEER.

My story, Sir Pen, is, to put it briefly :
I'm a blank sheet of paper that no one will write
on.

HUSSEIN.

No man understands in the least what I'm good
for ;
They all want to use me for scattering sand with !

PEER.

I was in a woman's keeping a silver-clasped
book ;—
It's one and the same misprint to be either mad
or sane !

HUSSEIN.

Just fancy, what an exhausting life .
To be a pen and never taste the edge of a knife !

PEER.
[*With a high leap.*]

Just fancy, for a reindeer to leap from on high—
To fall and fall—and never feel the ground
beneath your hoofs !

HUSSEIN.

A knife ! I am blunt ;—quick, mend me and slit
me !
The world will go to ruin if they don't mend my
point for me !

PEER.

A pity for the world which, like other self-made
things,
Was reckoned by the Lord to be so excellently
good.

BEGRIFFENFELDT.

Here's a knife!

HUSSEIN.

[*Seizing it.*]

Ah, how I shall lick up the ink now!
Oh, what rapture to cut oneself! [*Cuts his throat.*

BEGRIFFENFELDT.

[*Stepping aside.*]

Pray do not sputter.

PEER.

[*In increasing terror.*]

Hold him!

HUSSEIN.

Ay, hold me!   That is the word!
Hold!   Hold the pen!   On the desk with **the**
    paper——!   [*Falls.*
I'm outworn.   The postscript—remember it, pray :
He lived and he died as a fate-guided pen ¹

PEER.

[*Dizzily.*]

What shall I——! What am I? Thou mighty——
    hold fast!
I am all that thou wilt,—I'm a Turk, I'm a
    sinner——
A hill-troll——; but help;—there was something
    that burst——!   [*Shrieks.*
I cannot just hit on thy name at the moment ;—
Oh, come to my aid, thou—all madmen's protector!
                                [*Sinks down insensible.*

---

¹ "En påholden pen."   "Underskrive med påholden pen"—
to sign by touching a pen which is guided by another.

BEGRIFFENFELDT.

*[With a wreath of straw in his hand, gives a bound
and sits astride of him.]*

Ha! See him in the mire enthronëd;—
Beside himself—— To crown him now!

[Presses the wreath on PEER GYNT's *head,
and shouts :*

Long life, long life to Self-hood's Kaiser!

SCHAFMANN.

[In the cage.]

Es lebe hoch der grosse Peer !

ACT FIFTH.

SCENE FIRST.

On board a ship on the North Sea, off the Norwegian coast. Sunset. Stormy weather.

PEER GYNT, *a vigorous old man, with grizzled hair and beard, is standing aft on the poop. He is dressed half sailor-fashion, with a pea-jacket and long boots. His clothing is rather the worse for wear; he himself is weather-beaten, and has a somewhat harder expression. The* CAPTAIN *is standing beside the steersman at the wheel. The crew are forward.*

PEER GYNT.
[Leans with his arms on the bulwark, and gazes towards the land.]

Look at Hallingskarv[1] in his winter furs ;—
He's ruffling it, old one, in the evening glow.
The Jokel,[1] his brother, stands behind him askew ;
He's got his green ice-mantle still on his back.
The Folgefånn,[1] now, she is mighty fine,—
Lying there like a maiden in spotless white.
Don't you be madcaps, old boys that you are !
Stand where you stand ; you're but granite knobs.

THE CAPTAIN.
[Shouts forward.]

Two hands to the wheel, and the lantern aloft !

[1] Mountains and glaciers.

PEER.

It's blowing up stiff——

THE CAPTAIN.

——for a gale to-night.

PEER.

Can one see the Rondë Hills from the sea ?

THE CAPTAIN.

No, how should you ? They lie at the back of
the snowfields.

PEER.

Or Blåhö ?[1]

THE CAPTAIN.

No ; but from up in the rigging,
You've a glimpse, in clear weather, of Gald-
höpiggen.[1]

PEER.

Where does Hårteig[1] lie ?

THE CAPTAIN.

[*Pointing.*]

About over there.

PEER.

I thought so.

THE CAPTAIN.

You know where you are, it appears.

PEER.

When I left the country, I sailed by here ;
And the dregs, says the proverb, hang in to the
          last.   [*Spits, and gazes at the coast.*
In there, where the screes and the clefts lie blue,—

Mountains and glaciers.

Where the valleys, like trenches, gloom narrow
    and black,—
And underneath, skirting the open fiords,—
It's in places like these human beings abide.
                   [Looks at the CAPTAIN.
They build far apart in this country.

THE CAPTAIN.
                         Ay;
Few are the dwellings and far between.

PEER.
Shall we get in by day-break?

THE CAPTAIN.
                  Thereabouts;
If we don't have too dirty a night altogether.

PEER,
It grows thick in the west.

THE CAPTAIN.
               It does so.
PEER.
                Stop a bit!
You might put me in mind when we make up
    accounts—
I'm inclined, as the phrase goes, to do a good turn
To the crew——

THE CAPTAIN.
        I thank you.

PEER.
            It won't be much
I have dug for gold, and lost what I found;—

We are quite at loggerheads, Fate and I.
You know what I've got in safe keeping on board—
That's all I have left ;—the rest's gone to the devil.

THE CAPTAIN.

It's more than enough, though, to make you of
    weight
Among people at home here.

PEER.

          I've no relations.
There's no one awaiting the rich old curmudgeon.—
Well ; that saves you, at least, any scenes on the
    pier !

THE CAPTAIN.

Here comes the storm.

PEER.

        Well, remember then—
If any of your crew are in real need,
I won't look too closely after the money——

THE CAPTAIN.

That's kind.   They are most of them ill enough
    off ;
They have all got their wives and their children
    at home.
With their wages alone they can scarce make ends
    meet ;
But if they come home with some cash to the
    good,
It will be a return not forgot in a hurry.

PEER.

What do you say ?   Have they wives and children ?
Are they married ?

THE CAPTAIN.

     Married? Ay, every man of them.
But the one that is worst off of all is the cook ;
Black famine is ever at home in his house.

PEER.

Married? They've folks that await them at
    home ?
Folks to be glad when they come ? Eh ?

THE CAPTAIN.

                   Of course,
In poor people's fashion.

PEER.

         And come they one evening,
What then ?

THE CAPTAIN.

     Why, I daresay the goodwife will fetch
Something good for a treat——

PEER.

       And a light in the sconce ?

THE CAPTAIN.

Ay, ay, may be two ; and a dram to their supper.

PEER.

And there they sit snug ! There's a fire on the
    hearth !
They've their children about them ! The room's
    full of chatter;
Not one hears another right out to an end,
For the joy that is on them——!

THE CAPTAIN.
                    It's likely enough.
So it's really kind, as you promised just now,
To help eke things out.

PEER.
[*Thumping the bulwark.*]
                    I'll be damned if I do!
Do you think I am mad? Would you have me
    fork out
For the sake of a parcel of other folks' brats?
I've slaved much too sorely in earning my cash.
There's nobody waiting for old Peer Gynt.

THE CAPTAIN.
Well well; as you please then; your money's your
    own.

PEER.
Right! Mine it is, and no one else's.
We'll reckon as soon as your anchor is down!
Take my fare, in the cabin, from Panama here.
Then brandy all round to the crew. Nothing
    more.
If I give a doit more, slap my jaw for me, Captain.

THE CAPTAIN.
I owe you a quittance, and not a thrashing;—
But excuse me, the wind's blowing up to a gale.
        [*He goes forward. It has fallen dark;
        lights are lit in the cabin. The sea
        increases. Fog and thick clouds.*

PEER.
To have a whole bevy of youngsters at home;—
Still to dwell in their minds as a coming delight;—

To have others' thoughts follow you still on your
　　path !—
There's never a soul gives a thought to me.—
Lights in the sconces ! I'll put out those lights.
I will hit upon something !—I'll make them all
　　drunk ;—
Not one of the devils shall go sober ashore.
They shall all come home drunk to their children
　　and wives !
They shall curse ; bang the table till it rings
　　again,—
They shall scare those that wait for them out of
　　their wits ?
The goodwife shall scream and rush forth from
　　the house,—
Clutch her children along ! All their joy gone to
　　ruin !
　　　　　　[*The ship gives a heavy lurch ; he staggers
　　　　　　　and keeps his balance with difficulty.*
Why, that was a buffet and no mistake.
The sea's hard at labour, as though it were paid
　　for it ;—
It's still itself here on the coasts of the north ;—
A cross-sea, as wry and wrong-headed as ever——
　　　　　　　　　　　　　　　　　　[*Listens.*
Why, what can those screams be ?

THE LOOK-OUT.
[*Forward.*]
A wreck a-lee

THE CAPTAIN.
[*On the main deck, shouts.*]
Starboard your helm ! Bring her up to the
　　wind !

THE MATE.

Are there men on the wreck?

THE LOOK-OUT.

I can just see three!

PEER.

Quick! lower the stern boat——

THE CAPTAIN.

She'd fill ere she floated.
                              [Goes forward.

PEER.

Who can think of that now?
                              [To some of the crew.
                         If you're men, to the rescue!
What the devil, if you should get a bit of a duck-
    ing!

THE BOATSWAIN.

It's out of the question in such a sea.

PEER.

They are screaming again!   There's a lull in the
    wind.—
Cook, will you risk it?   Quick!   I will pay——

THE COOK.

No, not if you offered me twenty pounds-ster-
    ling [1]——

PEER.

You hounds!   You chicken-hearts!   Can you
    forget
These are men that have goodwives and children
    at home?
There they're sitting and waiting——

[1] So in original.

THE BOATSWAIN.

      Well, patience is wholesome.

THE CAPTAIN.

Bear away from that sea!

THE MATE.

      There the wreck capsized!

PEER.

All is silent of a sudden——!

THE BOATSWAIN.

      Were they married, as you think,
There are three new-baked widows even now in
    the world.

      [*The storm increases.* PEER GYNT *moves
      away aft.*

PEER.

There is no faith left among men any more,—
No Christianity,—well may they say it and write
    it ;—
Their good deeds are few and their prayers are
    still fewer,
And they pay no respect to the Powers above
    them.—
In a storm like to-night's, he's a terror, the Lord is.
These beasts should be careful, and think, what's
    the truth,
That it's dangerous playing with elephants ;—
And yet they must openly brave his displeasure !
I am no whit to blame ; for the sacrifice
I can prove I stood ready, my money in hand.
But how does it profit me?—What says the
    proverb ?
A conscience at ease is a pillow of down.

Oh ay, that is all very well on dry land,
But I'm blest if it matters a snuff on board ship,
When a decent man's out on the seas with such
    riff-raff.
At sea one can never be one's self;
One must go with the others from deck to keel;
If for boatswain and cook the hour of vengeance
    should strike,
I shall no doubt be swept to the deuce with the
    rest;—
One's personal welfare is clean set aside;—
One counts but as a sausage in slaughtering-
    time.—
  My mistake is this: I have been too meek;
And I've had no thanks for it after all.
Were I younger, I think I would shift the saddle,
And try how it answered to lord it awhile.
There is time enough yet! They shall know
    in the parish
That Peer has come sailing aloft o'er the seas!
I'll get back the farmstead by fair means or
    foul;—
I will build it anew; it shall shine like a palace.
But none shall be suffered to enter the hall!
They shall stand at the gateway, all twirling their
    caps;—
They shall beg and beseech—that they freely
    may do;
But none gets so much as a farthing of mine.
If I've had to howl 'neath the lashes of fate,
Trust me to find folks I can lash in my turn——

THE STRANGE PASSENGER.

[*Stands in the darkness at* PEER GYNT'S *side, and
    salutes him in friendly fashion.*]

Good evening!

PEER.

Good evening! What——? Who are you?

THE PASSENGER.
Your fellow-passenger, at your service.

PEER.
Indeed? I thought I was the only one.

THE PASSENGER.
A mistaken impression, which now is set right.

PEER.
But it's singular that, for the first time to-night,
I should see you——

THE PASSENGER.
I never come out in the day-time.

PEER.
Perhaps you are ill? You're as white as a
　　sheet——

THE PASSENGER.
No, thank you—my health is uncommonly good.

PEER.
What a raging storm!

THE PASSENGER.
Ay, a blessëd one, man!

PEER.
A blessëd one?

THE PASSENGER.
Sea's running high as houses.
Ah, one can feel one's mouth watering!

Just think of the wrecks that to-night will be
      shattered;—
And think, too, what corpses will drive ashore!

                    PEER.

Lord save us '
                    THE PASSENGER.
             Have ever you seen a man strangled,
Or hanged,—or drowned?

                    PEER.
             This is going too far——!

                    THE PASSENGER.
The corpses all laugh. But their laughter is
      forced;
And the most part are found to have bitten their
      tongues.
                    PEER.
Hold off from me——!

                    THE PASSENGER.
             Only one question, pray!
If we, for example, should strike on a rock,
And sink in the darkness——

                    PEER.
             You think there is danger?

                    THE PASSENGER.
I really don't know what I ought to say.
But suppose, now, I float and you go to the
      bottom——
                    PEER.
Oh, rubbish——

THE PASSENGER.

It's just a hypothesis.
But when one is placed with one foot in the grave,
One grows soft-hearted and open-handed——

PEER.

[*Puts his hand in his pocket.*]

Ho, money?

THE PASSENGER

No, no; but perhaps you would kindly
Make me a gift of your much-esteemed
    carcase——?

PEER.

This is too much!

THE PASSENGER.

No more than your body, you know!
To help my researches in science——

PEER.

Begone!

THE PASSENGER.

But think, my dear sir—the advantage is yours!
I'll have you laid open and brought to the light.
What I specially seek is the centre of dreams,—
And with critical care I'll look into your
    seams——

PEER.

Away with you!

THE PASSENGER.

Why, my dear sir—a drowned corpse——!

PEER.

Blasphemer! You're goading the rage of the storm!
I call it too bad!   Here it's raining and blowing,

A terrible sea on, and all sorts of signs
Of something that's likely to shorten our days;—
And you carry on so as to make it come quicker!

THE PASSENGER.

You're in no mood, I see, to negotiate further;
But time, you know, brings with it many a
      change——   [*Nods in a friendly fashion.*
We'll meet when you're sinking, if not before;
Perhaps I may then find you more in the humour.
                              [*Goes into the cabin.*

PEER.

Unpleasant companions these scientists are!
With their freethinking ways——
                    [*To the* BOATSWAIN, *who is passing.*
                    Hark, a word with you, friend!
That passenger?   What crazy creature is he?

THE BOATSWAIN.

I know of no passenger here but yourself.

PEER.

No others?   This thing's getting worse and worse.
          [*To the* SHIP'S BOY, *who comes out of the
          cabin.*
Who went down the companion just now?

THE BOY.

                              The ship's dog, sir!
                              [*Passes on.*
          THE LOOK-OUT.
          [*Shouts.*]
Land close ahead!
                    PEER.

          Where's my box?   Where's my trunk?
All the baggage on deck!

THE BOATSWAIN.
>   We have more to attend to !

PEER.

It was nonsense, captain !   'Twas only my joke ;—
As sure as I'm here I will help the cook——

THE CAPTAIN.

The jib's blown away !

THE MATE.
>   And there went the foresail !

THE BOATSWAIN.
> [*Shrieks from forward.*]

Breakers under the bow !

THE CAPTAIN.
>   She will go to shivers !
> [*The ship strikes.   Noise and confusion.*

SCENE SECOND.

Close under the land, among sunken rocks and surf.
The ship sinks.   The jolly-boat, with two men in
her, is seen for a moment through the scud.   A sea
strikes her ; she fills and upsets.   A shriek is heard ;
then all is silent for a while.   Shortly afterwards
the boat appears floating bottom upwards.
PEER GYNT *comes to the surface near the boat.*

PEER.

Help ! Help !   A boat ! Help ! I'll be drowned !
Save me, oh Lord—as saith the text !
> [*Clutches hold of the boat's keel.*

THE COOK.
[Comes up on the other side.]
Oh, Lord God—for my children's sake,
Have mercy!   Let me reach the land!
[Seizes hold of the keel.

PEER.

Let go!

THE COOK.
Let go!

PEER.
I'll strike!

THE COOK.
So'll I!

PEER.

I'll crush you down with kicks and blows!
Let go your hold!   She won't float two!

THE COOK.
I know it!   Yield!

PEER.
Yield you!

THE COOK.
Oh yes!
[They fight; one of the COOK's *hands is
disabled; he clings on with the other.*

PEER.
Off with that hand!

THE COOK.
Oh, kind sir—spare!
Think of my little ones at home

PEER.

I need my life far more than you,
For I am lone and childless still.

THE COOK.

Let go! You've lived, and I am young!

PEER.

Quick; haste you; sink;—you drag us down.

THE COOK.

Have mercy! Yield in heaven's name!
There's none to miss and mourn for you—
      [*His hands slips; he screams:*
I'm drowning!

PEER.
[*Seizing him.*]
      By this wisp of hair
I'll hold you; say your Lord's Prayer, quick!

THE COOK.

I can't remember; all turns black——

PEER.

Come, the essentials in a word——!

THE COOK.

Give us this day——!

PEER.

      Skip that part, Cook;
You'll get all you need, safe enough.

THE COOK.

Give us this day——

PEER.

  The same old song!
'Tis plain you were a cook in life——
  [*The* COOK *slips from his grasp.*

THE COOK.

 [*Sinking.*]
Give us this day our ——   [*Disappears.*

PEER.

  Amen, lad!
To the last gasp you were yourself.—
  [*Draws himself up on to the bottom of the
  boat.*
So long as there is life there's hope——

THE STRANGE PASSENGER.

 [*Catches hold of the boat.*]
Good morning!

PEER.

 Hoy!

THE PASSENGER.

  I heard you shout.—
It's pleasant finding you again.
Well? So my prophecy came true!

PEER.

Let go!   Let go!   'Twill scarce float one!

THE PASSENGER.

I'm striking out with my left leg.
I'll float, if only with their tips
My fingers rest upon this ledge.
But apropos: your body——

PEER.

  Hush!

THE PASSENGER.

The rest, of course, is done for, clean——

PEER.

No more!

THE PASSENGER.

Exactly as you please.   [*Silence.*

PEER.

Well?

THE PASSENGER.

I am silent.

PEER.

Satan's tricks!——

What now?

THE PASSENGER.

I'm waiting.

PEER.

[*Tearing his hair.*]

I'll go mad!——

What are you?

THE PASSENGER.

[*Nods.*]

Friendly.

PEER.

What else! Speak!

THE PASSENGER.

What think you? Do you know none other
That's like me?

PEER.

Do I know the devil——?

THE PASSENGER.

[*In a low voice.*]

Is it his way to light a lantern
For life's night-pilgrimage through fear?

PEER.

Ah, come! When once the thing's cleared up,
You'd seem a messenger of light?

THE PASSENGER.

Friend,—have you once in each half-year
Felt all the earnestness of dread? [1]

PEER.

Why, one's afraid when danger threatens;—
But all your words have double meanings.[2]

THE PASSENGER.

Ay, have you gained but once in life
The victory that is given in dread?

PEER.

[*Looks at him.*]

Came you to ope for me a door,
'Twas stupid not to come before.
What sort of sense is there in choosing
Your time when seas gape to devour one?

THE PASSENGER.

Were, then, the victory more likely
Beside your hearthstone, snug and quiet?

PEER.

Perhaps not; but your talk was quizzical.
How could you fancy it awakening?

[1] "Angst"—literally, "dread" or "terror"—probably means
here something like "conviction of sin." The influence of the
Danish theologian, Sören Kierkegård, may be traced in this
passage.   [2] Literally, "Are set on screws."

THE PASSENGER.

Where I come from, there smiles are prized
As highly as pathetic style.

PEER.

All has its time ; what fits the taxman,[1]
So says the text, would damn the bishop.

THE PASSENGER.

The host whose dust inurned has slumbered
Treads not on week-days the cothurnus.

PEER.

Avaunt thee, bugbear !   Man, begone !
I will not die !   I must ashore !

THE PASSENGER.

Oh, as for that, be reassured ;—
One dies not midmost of Act Five.   [*Glides away.*

PEER.

Ah, there he let it out at last ;—
He was a sorry moralist.

SCENE THIRD.

Churchyard in a high-lying mountain parish.
A funeral is going on.   By the grave, the PRIEST *and a*
   gathering of people.   The last verse of the psalm
   is being sung. PEER GYNT *passes by on the road.*

PEER.

[*At the gate.*]

Here's a countryman going the way of all flesh.
God be thanked that it isn't me.
                              [*Enters the churchyard.*

[1] " Tolder," the biblical "publican."

The Priest.
[Speaking beside the grave.]

Now, when the soul has gone to meet its doom,
And here the dust lies, like an empty pod,—
Now, my dear friends, we'll speak a word or two
About this dead man's pilgrimage on earth.

 He was not wealthy, neither was he wise,
His voice was weak, his bearing was unmanly,
He spoke his mind abashed and faltering,
He scarce was master at his own fireside ;
He sidled into church, as though appealing
For leave, like other men, to take his place.

 It was from Gudbrandsdale, you know, he came.
When here he settled he was but a lad ;—
And you remember how, to the very last,
He kept his right hand hidden in his pocket.

 That right hand in the pocket was the feature
That chiefly stamped his image on the mind,—
And therewithal his writhing, his abashed
Shrinking from notice wheresoe'er he went.

 But, though he still pursued a path aloof,
And ever seemed a stranger in our midst,
You all know what he strove so hard to hide,—
The hand he muffled had four fingers only.—

 I well remember, many years ago,
One morning ; there were sessions held at Lundë.
'Twas war-time, and the talk in every mouth
Turned on the country's sufferings and its fate.

 I stood there watching.   At the table sat
The Captain, 'twixt the Bailiff[1] and the sergeants ;
Lad after lad was measured up and down,
Passed, and enrolled, and taken for a soldier.
The room was full, and from the green outside,
Where thronged the young folks, loud the laughter
  rang.

[1] See footnote, p. 95.

A name was called, and forth another stepped,
One pale as snow upon the glacier's edge.
They bade the youth advance ; he reached the
     table ;
We saw his right hand swaddled in a clout ;—
He gasped, he swallowed, battling after words,—
But, though the Captain urged him, found no
     voice.
Ah yes, at last ! Then with his cheek aflame,
His tongue now failing him, now stammering fast
He mumbled something of a scythe that slipped
By chance, and shore his finger to the skin.
     Straightway a silence fell upon the room.
Men bandied   meaning   glances ;   they made
     mouths ;
They stoned the boy with looks of silent scorn.
He felt the hail-storm, but he saw it not.
Then up the Captain stood, the grey old man ;
He spat, and pointed forth, and thundered " Go ! "
     And the lad went.   On both sides men fell
     back,
Till through their midst he had to run the
     gauntlet.
He reached the door ; from there he took to
     flight ;—
Up, up he went,—through wood and over hillside,
Up through the stone-screes, rough, precipitous.
He had his home up there among the moun-
     tains.—
     It was some six months later he came here,
With mother, and betrothed, and little child.
He leased some ground upon the high hill-side,
There where the waste lands trend away towards
     Lomb.
He married the first moment that he could ;
He built a house ; he broke the stubborn soil ;

He throve, as many a cultivated patch
Bore witness, bravely clad in waving gold.
At church he kept his right hand in his pocket,—
But sure I am at home his fingers nine
Toiled every whit as hard as others' ten.—
One spring the torrent washed it all away.
    Their lives were spared. Ruined and stripped
      of all,
He set to work to make another clearing;
And, ere the autumn, smoke again arose
From a new, better-sheltered, mountain farm-
    house.
Sheltered? From torrent—not from avalanche;
Two years, and all beneath the snow lay buried.
    But still the avalanche could not daunt his
      spirit.
He dug, and raked, and carted—cleared the
    ground—
And the next winter, ere the snow-blasts came,
A third time was his little homestead reared.
    Three sons he had, three bright and stirring
      boys;
They must to school, and school was far away;—
And they must clamber, where the hill-track
    failed,
By narrow ledges past the headlong scree.
What did he do? The eldest had to manage
As best he might, and, where the path was worst,
His father bound a rope round him to stay him;—
The others on his back and arms he bore.
    Thus he toiled, year by year, till they were men.
Now might he well have looked for some return.
In the New World, three prosperous gentlemen
Their school-going and their father have forgotten.
    He was short-sighted. Out beyond the circle
Of those most near to him he nothing saw.

To him seemed meaningless as cymbals' tinkling
Those words that to the heart should ring like
    steel.
His race, his fatherland, all things high and
    shining,
Stood ever, to his vision, veiled in mist.
    But he was humble, humble, was this man;
And since that sessions-day his doom oppressed
    him,
As surely as his cheeks were flushed with shame,
And his four fingers hidden in his pocket.—
Offender 'gainst his country's laws?   Ay, true!
But there is one thing that the law outshineth
Sure as the snow-white tent of Glittertind [1]
Has clouds, like higher rows of peaks, above it.
No patriot was he.   Both for church and state
A fruitless tree.   But there, on the upland ridge,
In the small circle where he saw his calling,
There he was great, because he was himself.
His inborn note rang true unto the end.
His days were as a lute with muted strings.
And therefore, peace be with thee, silent warrior,
That fought the peasant's little fight, and fell!
    It is not ours to search the heart and reins;—
That is no task for dust, but for its ruler;—
Yet dare I freely, firmly, speak my hope:
He scarce stands crippled now before his God!
        [*The gathering disperses.* PEER GYNT
        remains behind, alone.

PEER.

Now that is what I call Christianity!
Nothing to seize on one's mind unpleasantly.—
And the topic—immovably being oneself,—

[1] A mountain in the Jotunheim.   The name means "glittering peak."

That the pastor's homily turned upon,—
Is full, in its essence, of edification.

> [*Looks down upon the grave.*

Was it he, I wonder, that hacked through his
    knuckle
That day I was out hewing logs in the forest?
Who knows? If I weren't standing here with my
    staff
By the side of the grave of this kinsman in spirit,
I could almost believe it was I that slept,
And heard in a vision my panegyric.—
It's a seemly and Christianlike custom indeed
This casting a so-called memorial glance
In charity over the life that is ended.
I shouldn't at all mind accepting my verdict
At the hands of this excellent parish priest.
Ah well, I dare say I have some time left
Ere the gravedigger comes to invite me to stay
    with him ;—
And as Scripture has it : What's best is best,—
And : Enough for the day is the evil thereof,— [1]
and further : Discount not thy funeral.—
Ah, the Church, after all, is the true consoler.
I've hitherto scarcely appreciated it ;—
But now I feel clearly how blessëd it is
To be well assured upon sound authority :
Even as thou sowest thou shalt one day reap.—
One must be oneself; for oneself and one's own
One must do one's best, both in great and in small
    things.
If the luck goes against you, at least you've the
    honour
Of a life carried through in accordance with
    principle.—

---

[1] "Den tid den sorg"—literally, "That time that sorrow" or "care."

Now homewards!   Though narrow and steep the
   path,
Though fate to the end may be never so biting—
Still old Peer Gynt will pursue his own way,
And remain what he is: poor, but virtuous ever.
                                   [*Goes out.*

SCENE FOURTH.

*A hill-side seamed by the dry bed of a torrent.   A
   ruined mill-house beside the stream.   The ground
   is torn up, and the whole place waste.   Further
   up the hill, a large farm-house.*
*An auction is going on in front of the farm-house.
   There is a great gathering of people, who are
   drinking, with much noise.   PEER GYNT is sitting on a rubbish-heap beside the mill.*

PEER.

Forward and back, and it's just as far;
Out and in, and it's just as strait.—
Time wears away and the river gnaws on.
Go roundabout, the Boyg said;—and here one must.

A MAN DRESSED IN MOURNING.

Now there is only rubbish left over.
                     [*Catches sight of* PEER GYNT.
Are there strangers here too ?   God be with you,
   good friend !

PEER.

Well met !   You have lively times here to-day.
Is't a christening junket or wedding feast ?

THE MAN IN MOURNING.

I'd rather call it a house-warming treat;—
The bride is laid in a wormy bed.

PEER.

And the worms are squabbling for rags and clouts.

THE MAN IN MOURNING.

That's the end of the ditty ; it's over and done.

PEER.

All the ditties end just alike ;
And they're all old together ; I knew 'em as a boy

A LAD OF TWENTY.

[*With a casting-ladle.*]

Just look what a rare thing I've been buying !
In this Peer Gynt cast his silver buttons.

ANOTHER.

Look at mine, though !   The money-bag [1] bought
for a halfpenny.

A THIRD.

No more, eh ?   Twopence for the pedlar's pack !

PEER.

Peer Gynt ?   Who was he ?

THE MAN IN MOURNING.

All I know is this :
He was kinsman to Death and to Aslak the
Smith.

A MAN IN GREY.

You're forgetting me, man !   Are you mad or
drunk ?

THE MAN IN MOURNING.

You forget that at Hegstad was a storehouse door.

[1] Literally, "the bushel."   See note, p. 11.

THE MAN IN GREY.

Ay, true ; but we know you were never dainty.

THE MAN IN MOURNING.

If only she doesn't give Death the slip——

THE MAN IN GREY.

Come, kinsman !   A dram, for our kinship's sake !

THE MAN IN MOURNING.

To the deuce with your kinship!   You're maunder-
ing in drink——

THE MAN IN GREY.

Oh, rubbish ; blood's never so thin as all that ;
One cannot but feel one's akin to Peer Gynt.

[*Goes off with him.*

PEER.

[*To himself.*]

One meets with acquaintances,

A LAD.

[*Calls after the* MAN IN MOURNING.]

Mother that's dead
Will be after you, Aslak, if you wet your whistle.

PEER.

[*Rises.*]

The husbandman's saying seems scarce to hold here:
The deeper one harrows the better it smells.

A LAD.

[*With a bear's skin.*]

Look, the cat of the Dovrë ! [1]   Well, only his fell,
It was he chased the trolls out on Christmas Eve.

See Appendix.

ANOTHER.

[*With a reindeer skull.*]

Here is the wonderful reindeer that bore,
At Gendin, Peer Gynt over edge and scree.

A THIRD.

[*With a hammer, calls out to the* MAN IN MOURNING.]

Hei, Aslak, this sledge-hammer, say, do you know
  it ?

Was it this that you used when the devil clove
  the wall ?

A FOURTH.

[*Empty-handed.*]

Mads Moen, here's the invisible cloak
Peer Gynt and Ingrid flew off through the air
  with.

PEER.

Brandy here, boys !   I feel I'm grown old ;—
I must put up to auction my rubbish and lumber !

A LAD.

What have you to sell, then ?

PEER.

A palace I have ;—
It lies in the Rondë ; it's solidly built.

THE LAD.

A button is bid !

PEER.

You must run to a dram.
'Twere a sin and a shame to bid anything less.

ANOTHER.

He's a jolly old boy this !

[*The bystanders crowd around him.*

PEER.
[*Shouts.*]

Granë,[1] my steed ;

Who bids ?

ONE OF THE CROWD.
Where's he running ?

PEER.

Why, far in the west !
Near the sunset, my lads ! Ah, that courser can
     fly
As fast, ay, as fast as Peer Gynt could lie.

VOICES.
What more have you got ?

PEER.

I've both rubbish and gold !
I bought it with ruin ; I'll sell it at a loss.

A LAD.

Put it up !

PEER.
A dream of a silver-clasped book !
That you can have for an old hook and eye.

THE LAD.
To the devil with dreams !

PEER.

Here's my Kaiserdom !
I throw it in the midst of you ; scramble for it !

THE LAD.
Is the crown given in ?

See footnote, p. 114.

PEER.
                        Of the loveliest straw.
It will fit whoever first puts it on.
Hei, there is more yet !   An addled egg !
A madman's grey hair ! And the Prophet's
    beard !
All these shall be his that will show on the hillside
A post that has writ on it ; Here lies your path !

THE BAILIFF.[1]
[*Who has come up.*]
You're carrying on, my good man, so that almost
I think that your path will lead straight to the
    lock-up.
PEER.
[*Hat in hand.*]
Quite likely.   But, tell me, who was Peer Gynt ?

THE BAILIFF.
Oh, nonsense——

PEER.
        Your pardon !   Most humbly I beg——!

THE BAILIFF.
Oh, he's said to have been an abominable liar——[2]

PEER.
A liar—— ?

THE BAILIFF.
            Yes—all that was strong and great
He made believe always that he had done it.
But, excuse me, friend—I have other duties——
                                        [*Goes.*

[1] See footnote, p. 95.
[2] "Digter"; means also "poet."

PEER.

And where is he now, this remarkable man?

AN ELDERLY MAN.

He fared over seas to a foreign land;
It went ill with him there, as one well might
    foresee;—
It's many a year now since he was hanged.

PEER.

Hanged: Ay, ay! Why, I thought as much;
Our lamented Peer Gynt was himself to the last.
                                    [*Bows.*
Good-bye,—and best thanks for to-day's merry
    meeting.
              [*Goes a few steps, but stops again.*
You joyous youngsters, you comely lasses,—
Shall I pay my shot with a traveller's tale?

SEVERAL VOICES.

Yes; do you know any?

PEER.

            Nothing more easy.—
       [*He comes nearer; a look of strangeness
            comes over him.*
I was gold-digging once in San Francisco.
There were mountebanks swarming all over the
    town.
One with his toes could perform on the fiddle;
Another could dance a Spanish halling[1] on his
    knees;
A third, I was told, kept on making verses
While his brain-pan was having a hole bored
    right through it.

[1] See footnotes, pp. 29 and 30.

To the mountebank-meeting came also the
　　devil ;—
Thought he'd try his luck with the rest of them.
His talent was this : in a manner convincing,
He was able to grunt like a flesh-and-blood pig.
He was not recognised, yet his manners[1] attracted.
The house was well filled ; expectation ran high.
He stepped forth in a cloak with an ample cape
　　to it ;
Man mus sich drappiren, as the Germans say.
But under the mantle—what none suspected—
He'd managed to smuggle a real live pig.
And now he opened the representation ;
The devil he pinched, and the pig gave voice.
The whole thing purported to be a fantasia
On the porcine existence, both free and in bonds ;
And all ended up with a slaughter-house squeal—
Whereupon the performer bowed low and retired.—
The critics discussed and appraised the affair ;
The tone of the whole was attacked and defended.
Some fancied the vocal expression too thin,
While some thought the death-shriek too care-
　　fully studied ;
But all were agreed as to one thing : *qua* grunt,
The performance was grossly exaggerated.—
Now that, you see, came of the devil's stupidity
In not taking the measure of his public first.
　　　　[*He bows and goes off. A puzzled silence
　　　　　comes over the crowd.*

　　　In the original, " Personlighed "—personality.

SCENE FIFTH.

Whitsun Eve.—In the depths of the forest. To the back, in a clearing, is a hut with a pair of reindeer horns over the porch-gable.
PEER GYNT *is creeping among the undergrowth, gathering wild onions.*

PEER.

Well, this is one standpoint.   Where is the next?
One should try all things and choose the best.
Well, I have done so,—beginning from Cæsar,
And downwards as far as to Nebuchadnezzar.
So I've had, after all, to go through Bible history;—
The old boy has come back to his mother again.
After all it is written: Of the earth art thou
      come.—
The main thing in life is to fill one's belly.
Fill it with onions?   That's not much good ;—
I must take to cunning, and set out snares.
There's water in the beck here; I shan't suffer
      thirst ;
And I count as the first 'mong the beasts after all.
When my time comes to die—as most likely it
      will,—
I shall crawl in under a wind-fallen tree ;
Like the bear, I will heap up a leaf-mound above
      me,
And I'll scratch in big print on the bark of the
      tree :
Here rests Peer Gynt, that decent soul
Kaiser o'er all of the other beasts.—
Kaiser ?   [*Laughs inwardly.*
      Why, you old soothsayer's-dupe !

No Kaiser are you ; you are nought but an onion.
I'm going to peel you now, my good Peer !
You won't escape either by begging or howling.

> [*Takes an onion and strips off one coat*
> *after another.*

There lies the outermost layer, all torn ;
That's the shipwrecked man on the jolly-boat's
    keel.
Here's the passenger layer, scanty and thin ;—
And yet in its taste there's a tang of Peer Gynt.
Next underneath is the gold-digger ego ;
The juice is all gone—if it ever had any.
This coarse-grained layer with the hardened skin
Is the peltry hunter by Hudson's Bay.
The next one looks like a crown ;—oh, thanks !
We'll throw it away without more ado.
Here's the archæologist, short but sturdy ,
And here is the Prophet, juicy and fresh.
He stinks, as the Scripture has it, of lies,
Enough to bring the water to an honest man's
    eyes.
This layer that rolls itself softly together
Is the gentleman, living in ease and good cheer.
The next one seems sick.   There are black streaks
    upon it ;—
Black symbolises both parsons and niggers.

> [*Pulls off several layers at once.*

What an enormous number of swathings !
Is not the kernel soon coming to light ?

> [*Pulls the whole onion to pieces.*

I'm blest if it is !   To the innermost centre,
It's nothing but swathings—each smaller and
    smaller.—
Nature is witty !   [*Throws the fragments away.*
    The devil take brooding !
If one goes about thinking, one's apt to stumble.

Well, *I* can at any rate laugh at that danger;—
For here on all fours I am firmly planted.
                              [*Scratches his head.*
A queer enough business, the whole concern !
Life, as they say, plays with cards up its sleeve ; [1]
But when one snatches at them, they've dis-
      appeared,
And one grips something else,—or else nothing
      at all.
            [*He has come near to the hut ; he catches
            sight of it and starts.*
This hut ?   On the heath——!   Ha !
                              [*Rubs his eyes.*
                        It seems exactly
As though I had known this same building
      before.—
The reindeer-horns jutting above the gable !—
A mermaid, shaped like a fish from the navel !—
Lies ! there's no mermaid !   But nails—and
      planks,—
Bars too, to shut out hobgoblin thoughts ·—

                    SOLVEIG.
            [*Singing in the hut.*]
      Now all is ready for Whitsun Eve.
      Dearest boy of mine, far away,
            Comest thou soon ?
            Is thy burden heavy,
            Take time, take time ;—
            I will await thee ;
            I promised of old.[2]

[1] This and the following line, literally translated, run thus :
Life, as it's called, has a fox behind its ear.   But when one
grasps at him, Reynard takes to his heels."   "To have a fox
behind the ear" is a proverbial expression for insincerity,
double-dealing.
[2] See footnote, p. 171.

PEER.

[Rises, quiet and deadly pale.]

One that's remembered,—and one that's forgot.

One that has squandered,—and one that has
    saved.—

Oh, earnest!—and never can the game be played
    o'er!

Oh, dread! [1]—here was my Kaiserdom!

> *[Hurries off along the wood path.*

SCENE SIXTH.

*Night.   A heath, with fir-trees.   A forest fire has
    been raging; charred tree-trunks are seen stretch-
    ing for miles.   White mists here and there
    clinging to the earth.*

PEER GYNT *comes running over the heath.*

PEER.

Ashes, fog-scuds, dust wind-driven,—
Here's enough for building with!
Stench and rottenness within it;
All a whited sepulchre.
Figments, dreams, and still born knowledge
Lay the pyramid's foundation;
O'er them shall the work mount upwards,
With its step on step of falsehood.
Earnest shunned, repentance dreaded,
Flaunt at the apex like a scutcheon,
Fill the trump of judgment with their:
" Petrus Gyntus Cæsar fecit!"   *[Listens*
What is this, like children's weeping?
Weeping, but half-way to song.—

---

[1] See footnote, p. 21.

Thread-balls[1] at my feet are rolling !—
                              [*Kicking at them.*
Off with you !   You block my path !

THE THREAD-BALLS.
[*On the ground.*]
We are thoughts ;
Thou shouldst have thought us ;—
Feet to run on
Thou shouldst have given us !

PEER.
[*Going round about.*]
I have given life to one ;—
'Twas a bungled, crook-legged thing !

THE THREAD-BALLS.
We should have soared up
Like clangorous voices,—
And here we must trundle
As grey-yarn thread-balls.

PEER.
[*Stumbling.*]
Thread-clue !   you accursed scamp !
Would you trip your father's heels ?   [*Flees.*

WITHERED LEAVES.
[*Flying before the wind.*]
We are a watchword ;
Thou shouldst have proclaimed us !
See how thy dozing
Has wofully riddled us.
The worm has gnawed us

See Introduction.

In every crevice;
We have never twined us
Like wreaths round fruitage.

PEER.

Not in vain your birth, however;—
Lie but still and serve as manure.

A SIGHING IN THE AIR.

We are songs;
Thou shouldst have sung us!—
A thousand times over
Hast thou cowed us and smothered us.
Down in thy heart's pit
We have lain and waited;—
We were never called forth.
Thy gorge we poison!

PEER.

Poison thee, thou foolish stave!
Had I time for verse and stuff?

[*Attempts a short cut.*

DEWDROPS.

[*Dripping from the branches.*]

We are tears
Unshed for ever.
Ice-spears, sharp-wounding,
We could have melted.
Now the barb rankles
In the shaggy bosom;—
The wound is closed over;
Our power is ended.

PEER.

Thanks;—I wept in Rondë-cloisters,—
None the less my tail-part smarted!

Broken Straws.

We are deeds;
Thou shouldst have achieved us!
Doubt, the throttler,
Has crippled and riven us.
On the Day of Judgment
We'll come a-flock,
And tell the story,—
Then woe to you!

Peer.

Rascal-tricks!   How dare you debit
What is negative against me ?   [*Hastens away.*

Åse's Voice.
[*Far away.*]

Fie, what a post-boy!
Hu, you've upset me
Here in the slush, boy!
Sadly it's smirched me.—
You've driven me the wrong way.
Peer, where's the castle?
The Fiend has misled you
With the switch from the cupboard

Peer.

Better haste away, poor fellow!
With the devil's sins upon you,
Soon you'll faint upon the hillside ;—
Hard enough to bear one's own sins.   [*Runs off.*

SCENE SEVENTH.

Another part of the heath.

PEER GYNT.
[*Sings.*]

A sexton! A sexton! where are you, hounds?
A song from braying precentor-mouths;
Around your hat-brim a mourning band;—
My dead are many; I must follow their biers!

THE BUTTON-MOULDER, *with a box of tools and a large casting-ladle, comes from a side path.*

THE BUTTON-MOULDER.

Well met, old gaffer!

PEER.

Good evening, friend!

THE BUTTON-MOULDER.

The man's in a hurry. Why, where is he going?

PEER.

To a grave-feast.

THE BUTTON-MOULDER.

Indeed? My sight's not very good;—
Excuse me,—your name doesn't chance to be
    Peer?

PEER.

Peer Gynt, as the saying is.

THE BUTTON-MOULDER.

That I call luck!
It's precisely Peer Gynt I am sent for to-night.

PEER.

You're sent for ?   What do you want ?

THE BUTTON-MOULDER.

Why, see here ;
I mould buttons ; and you must go into my
    ladle.

PEER.

What to do there ?

THE BUTTON-MOULDER.

To be melted up.

PEER.

To be melted ?

THR BUTTON-MOULDER.

Here it is, empty and scoured.
Your grave is dug ready, your coffin bespoke.
The worms in your body will live at their ease ;—
But I have orders, without delay,
On Master's behalf to fetch in your soul.

PEER.

It can't be !   Like this, without any warning——!

THE BUTTON-MOULDER.

It's an old tradition at burials and births
To appoint in secret the day of the feast,
With no warning at all to the guest of honour.

PEER.

Ay, ay, that's true.   All my brain's awhirl.
You are—— ?

THE BUTTON-MOULDER.

Why, I told you—a button-moulder.

PEER.

I see !   A pet child has many nicknames.
So that's it, Peer ; it is there you're to harbour
But these, my good man, are most unfair pro-
     ceedings !
I'm sure I deserve better treatment than this ;—
I'm not nearly so bad as perhaps you think,—
Indeed I've done more or less good in the world ;—
At worst you may call me a sort of a bungler,—
But certainly not an exceptional sinner.

THE BUTTON-MOULDER.

Why that is precisely the rub, my man ;
You're no sinner at all in the higher sense ;
That's why you're excused all the torture-pangs,
And, like others, land in the casting-ladle.

PEER.

Give it what name you please—call it ladle or
     pool ;[1]
Spruce ale and swipes, they are both of them
     beer.
Avaunt from me, Satan !

THE BUTTON-MOULDER.

                    You can't be so rude
As to take my foot for a horse's hoof ?

PEER.

On horse's hoof or on fox's claws [2]—
Be off ; and be careful what you're about !

THE BUTTON-MOULDER.

My friend, you're making a great mistake.

---

[1] "Pöl," otherwise "Svovlpöl"—the sulphur pool of hell
[2] See footnote, p. 229.

We're both in a hurry, and so, to save time,
I'll explain the reason of the whole affair.
You are, with your own lips you told me so,
No sinner on the so-called heroic scale,—
Scarce middling even——

PEER.

Ah, now you're beginning
To talk common sense——

THE BUTTON-MOULDER.

Just have patience a bit—
But to call you a good man were going too far.—

PEER.

Well, you know I have never laid claim to that.

THE BUTTON-MOULDER.

You're nor one thing nor t'other then, only so-so.
A sinner of really grandiose style
Is nowadays not to be met on the highways.
It wants much more than merely to wallow in mire;
For both vigour and earnestness go to a sin.

PEER.

Ay, it's very true that remark of yours ;
One has to lay on, like the old Berserkers.

THE BUTTON-MOULDER

You, friend, on the other hand, took your sin
lightly.

PEER.

Only outwardly, friend, like a splash of mud.

THE BUTTON-MOULDER.

Ah, we'll soon be at one now.   The sulphur pool
Is no place for you, who but plashed in the mire.

PEER.

And in consequence, friend, I may go as I came?

THE BUTTON-MOULDER.

No, in consequence, friend, I must melt you up.

PEER.

What tricks are these that you've hit upon
At home here, while I've been in foreign parts?

THE BUTTON-MOULDER.

The custom's as old as the Snake's creation;
It's designed to prevent loss of good material.
You've worked at the craft—you must know that
   often
A casting turns out, to speak plainly, mere dross;
The buttons, for instance, have sometimes no loop
   to them.
What did you do then?

PEER.

                    Flung the rubbish away.

THE BUTTON-MOULDER.

Ah, yes; Jon Gynt was well known for a waster,
So long as he'd aught left in wallet or purse.
But Master, you see, he is thrifty, he is;
And that is why he's so well-to-do.
He flings nothing away as entirely worthless
That can be made use of as raw material.
Now, you were designed for a shining button
On the vest of the world; but your loop gave
   way;
So into the waste-box you needs must go,
And then, as they phrase it, be merged in the
   mass.

PEER.

You're surely not meaning to melt me up,
With Dick, Tom, and Hal,[1] into something new?

THE BUTTON-MOULDER.

That just what I do mean, and nothing else.
We've done it already to plenty of folks.
At Kongsberg [2] they do just the same with coin
That's been current so long that its impress is
    lost.

PEER.

But this is the wretchedest miserliness!
My dear good friend, let me get off free;—
A loopless button, a worn out farthing,—
What is that to a man in your Master's position?

THE BUTTON-MOULDER.

Oh, so long as, and seeing, the spirit is in you,
You always have value as so much metal.

PEER.

No, I say! No! With both teeth and claws
I'll fight against this! Sooner anything else!

THE BUTTON-MOULDER.

But what else? Come now, be reasonable.
You know you're not airy enough for heaven——

PEER.

I'm not hard to content; I don't aim so high;—
But I won't be deprived of one doit of my Self.

   [1] Literally, "With Peter and Paul."
   [2] The Royal Mint is at Kongsberg, a town in southern
Norway.

Have me judged by the law in the old-fashioned
     way !
For a certain time place me with Him of the Hoof;—
Say a hundred years, come the worst to the worst;
That, now, is a thing that one surely can bear;
They say that the torment is moral no more,
So it can't be so pyramid-like after all.
It is, as 'tis written, a mere transition ;
And as the fox said : One waits; there comes
An hour of deliverance ; one lives in seclusion,
And hopes in the meantime for happier days.—
But this other notion—to have to be merged,
Like a mote, in the carcass of some outsider,—
This casting-ladle business, this Gynt-cessation,—
It stirs up my innermost soul in revolt !

The Button-moulder.

Bless me, my dear Peer, there is surely no need
To get so wrought up about trifles like this.
Yourself you never have been at all ;—
Then what does it matter, your dying right out ?

Peer.

Have *I* not been——?   I could almost laugh !
Peer Gynt, then, has been something else, I sup-
     pose!
No, Button-moulder, you judge in the dark.
If you could but look into my very reins,
You'd find only Peer there, and Peer all
     through,—
Nothing else in the world, no, nor anything more.

The Button-moulder.

It's impossible.   Here I have got my orders.
Look, here it is written : Peer Gynt shalt thou
     summon.

He has set at defiance his life's design ;
Clap him into the ladle with other spoilt goods.

PEER.

What nonsense ! They must mean some other
    person.
Is it really Peer ? It's not Rasmus, or Jon ?

THE BUTTON-MOULDER.

It is many a day since I melted them.
So come quietly now, and don't waste my time.

PEER.

I'll be damned if I do ! Ay, 'twould be a fine
    thing
If it turned out to-morrow some one else was
    meant.
You'd better take care what you're at, my good
    man !
Think of the onus you're taking upon you——

THE BUTTON-MOULDER.

I have it in writing——

PEER.

                    At least give me time

THE BUTTON-MOULDER.

What good would that do you ?

PEER.

                    I'll use it to prove
That I've been myself all the days of my life ;
And that's the question that's in dispute.

THE BUTTON-MOULDER.

You ll prove it ? And how ?

PEER.

Why, by vouchers and witnesses.

THE BUTTON-MOULDER.

I'm sadly afraid Master will not accept them.

PEER.

Impossible!   However, enough for the day[1]—!
My dear man, allow me a loan of myself;
I'll be back again shortly.   One is born only once,
And one's self, as created, one fain would stick to.
Come, are we agreed?

THE BUTTON-MOULDER.

Very well then, so be it.
But remember, we meet at the next cross-roads.
                              [PEER GYNT *runs off.*

SCENE EIGHTH.

A further point on the heath.

PEER.

[*Running hard.*]
Time is money, as the Scripture says.
If I only knew where the cross-roads are ;—
They may be near and they may be far.
The earth burns beneath me like red-hot iron.
A witness!   A witness!   Oh, where shall I find
      one?
It's almost unthinkable here in the forest.
The world is a bungle!   A wretched arrangement,
When a right must be proved that is patent as
      day!

See footnote, p. 218.

An OLD MAN, *bent with age, with a staff in his hand
and a bag on his back, is trudging in front of
him.*

THE OLD MAN.
[*Stops.*]

Dear, kind sir—a trifle to a houseless soul !

PEER.

Excuse me ; I've got no small change in my
    pocket——

THE OLD MAN.

Prince Peer ! Oh, to think we should meet
    again—— !

PEER.

Who are you ?

THE OLD MAN.
You forget the Old Man in the Rondë ?

PEER.

Why, you're never—— ?

THE OLD MAN.
The King of the Dovrë, my boy !

PEER.

The Dovrë-King ? Really ? The Dovrë-King ?
    Speak !

THE OLD MAN.

Oh, I've come terribly down in the world—— !

PEER.

Ruined ?

THE OLD MAN.
Ay, plundered of every stiver.
Here am I tramping it, starved as a wolf.

PEER.

Hurrah! Such a witness doesn't grow on the trees

THE OLD MAN.

My Lord Prince, too, has grizzled a bit since we met.

PEER.

My dear father-in-law, the years gnaw and wear
      one.—
Well well, a truce to all private affairs,—
And pray, above all things, no family jars.
I was then a sad madcap——

THE OLD MAN.

                    Oh yes ; oh yes ;—
His Highness was young ; and what won't one do
      then?
But his Highness was wise in rejecting his bride
He saved himself thereby both worry and shame
For since then she's utterly gone to the bad——

PEER.

Indeed !

THE OLD MAN.

          She has led a deplorable life ; [1]
And, just think,—she and Trond are now living
      together.

PEER.

Which Trond?

THE OLD MAN.

Of the Valfjeld.

PEER.

                    It's he? Aha ;
It was he I cut out with the sæter-girls.

[1] " Hun gik nu for koldt vand og lud "—literally, " to live on
cold water and lye "—to live wretchedly and be badly treated.

The Old Man.

But my grandson has shot up both stout and
tall,
And has flourishing children all over the
land——

Peer.

Now, my dear man, spare us this flow of words ;—
I've something quite different troubling my
mind.—
I've got into rather a ticklish position,
And am greatly in need of a witness or voucher ;—
That's how you could help me best, father-in-
law,
And I'll find you a trifle to drink my health.

The Old Man.

You don't say so ; can I be of use to his Highness ?
You'll give me a character, then, in return ?

Peer.

Most gladly. I'm somewhat hard pressed for
cash,
And must cut down expenses in every direction.
Now hear what's the matter. No doubt you
remember
That night when I came to the Rondë a-
wooing——

The Old Man.

Why, of course, my Lord Prince !

Peer.

Oh, no more of the Prince !
But no matter. You wanted, by sheer brute
force,
To bias my sight, with a slit in the lens,

And to change me about from Peer Gynt to a
    troll.
What did *I* do then ?   I stood out against it,—
Swore I would stand on no feet but my own ;
Love, power, and glory at once I renounced,
And all for the sake of remaining myself.
Now this fact, you see, you must swear to in
    Court——

THE OLD MAN.

No, I'm blest if I can.

PEER.

                Why, what nonsense is this ?

THE OLD MAN.

You surely don't want to compel me to lie ?
You pulled on the troll-breeches, don't you
    remember,
And tasted the mead——

PEER.

            Ay, you lured me seductively ;—
But I flatly declined the decisive test,
And that is the thing you must judge your man
    by.
It's the end of the ditty that all depends on.

THE OLD MAN.

But it ended, Peer, just in the opposite way.

PEER.

What rubbish is this ?

THE OLD MAN.

            When you left the Rondë,
You inscribed my motto upon your escutcheon.[1]

[1] Literally, " Wrote my motto behind your ear."

PEER.

What motto?

THE OLD MAN.

The potent and sundering word.

PEER.

The word?

THE OLD MAN.

That which severs the whole race of men
From the troll-folk: Troll! To thyself be
    enough!

PEER.

[Recoils a step.]

Enough!

THE OLD MAN.

And with every nerve in your body,
You've been living up to it ever since.

PEER.

What, I? Peer Gynt?

THE OLD MAN.

[Weeps.]

It's ungrateful of you!
You've lived as a troll, but have still kept it
    secret.
The word I taught you has shown you the way
To swing yourself up as a man of substance;—
And now you must needs come and turn up your
    nose
At me and the word you've to thank for it all.

PEER.

Enough! A hill-troll! An egoist!
This must be all rubbish; that's perfectly certain

The Old Man.

[Pulls out a bundle of old newspapers.]

I daresay you think we don't take in the papers?
Wait; here I'll show you in red and black [1]
How the " Bloksberg Post " eulogises you ;
And the " Heklefjeld Journal " has done the same
Ever since the winter you left the country.—
Do you care to read them ? You're welcome
    Peer.
Here's an article, look you, signed " Stallion-
    hoof."
And here too is one : " On Troll-Nationalism."
The writer points out and lays stress on the truth
That horns and a tail are of little importance,
So long as one has but a strip of the hide.
" Our enough," he concludes, " gives the hall-
    mark of trolldom
To man,"—and proceeds to cite you as an instance.

Peer.

A hill-troll ? I ?

The Old Man.

       Yes, that's perfectly clear.

Peer.

Might as well have stayed quietly where I was ?
Might have stayed in the Rondë in comfort and
    peace ?
Saved my trouble and toil and no end of shoe-
    leather ?
Peer Gynt—a troll ? Why, it's rubbish ! It's
    stuff !
Good-bye !   There's a halfpenny to buy you
    tobacco.

     [1] Clearly the troll-substitute for " in black and white."

THE OLD MAN.

Nay, my good Prince Peer!

PEER.

                    Let me go !   You're mad,
Or else doting.   Off to the hospital with you !

THE OLD MAN.

Oh, that is exactly what I'm in search of.
But, as I told you, my grandson's offspring
Have become overwhelmingly strong in the land,
And they say that I only exist in books.
The saw says : One's kin are unkindest of all ;
I've found to my cost that that saying is true.
It's cruel to count as mere figment and fable——

PEER.

My dear man, there are others who share the same
    fate.

THE OLD MAN.

And ourselves we've no Mutual Aid Society,
No alms-box or Penny Savings Bank ;—
In the Rondë, of course, they'd be out of place,

PEER.

No, that curs'd : To th'yself be enough was the
    word there !

THE OLD MAN.

Oh, come now, the Prince can't complain of the
    word.
And if he could manage by hook or by crook——

PEER.

My man, you have got on the wrong scent
    entirely ;

I'm myself, as the saying goes, fairly cleaned
    out[1]——

THE OLD MAN.

You surely can't mean it? His Highness a
    beggar?

PEER.

Completely.   His Highness's ego's in pawn.
And it's all your fault, you accursëd trolls!
That's what comes of keeping bad company.

THE OLD MAN.

So there came my hope toppling down from its
    perch again!
Good-bye!   I had best struggle on to the
    town——

PEER.

What would you do there?

THE OLD MAN.

                    I will go to the theatre.
The papers are clamouring for national talents——

PEER.

Good luck on your journey; and greet them from
    me.
If I can but get free, I will go the same way.
.A farce I will write them, a mad and profound
    one;
It's name shall be : "Sic transit gloria mundi."
            [*He runs off along the road; the* OLD MAN
            shouts after him.

---

[1] Literally, " On a naked hiĦ."

SCENE NINTH.

[At a cross-road.]

PEER GYNT.

Now comes the pinch, Peer, as never before !
This Dovrish E n o u g h has passed judgment upon
  you.
The vessel's a wreck ; one must float with the
  spars.
All else ; but to go to the scrap-heap—no, no !

THE BUTTON-MOULDER.
[At the cross-road.]

Well now, Peer Gynt, have you found your
  voucher?

PEER.

Is this, then, the cross-road ? Well, that is
  short work !

THE BUTTON-MOULDER.

I can see on your face, as it were on a signboard,
The gist of the paper before I have read it.

PEER.

I got tired of the hunt;—one might lose one's
  way——

THE BUTTON-MOULDER.

Yes ; and what does it lead to, after all ?

PEER.

True enough ; in the wood, and by night as
  well——

THE BUTTON-MOULDER.

There's an old man, though, trudging.   Shall we
    call him here ?

PEER.

No, let him go.   He is drunk, my dear fellow '

THE BUTTON-MOULDER.

But perhaps he might——

PEER.

           Hush ; no—let him alone !

THE BUTTON-MOULDER.

Well, shall we begin then ?

PEER.

         One question—just one :
What is it, at bottom, this " being oneself " ?

THE BUTTON-MOULDER.

A singular question, most odd in the mouth
Of a man who but now——

PEER.

        Come, a straightforward answer.

THE BUTTON-MOULDER.

To be oneself is : to slay oneself.
But on you that answer is doubtless lost ;
And therefore we'll say : to stand forth every-
    where
With Master's intention displayed like a sign-
    board.

PEER.

But suppose a man never has come to know
What Master meant with him?

THE BUTTON-MOULDER.

He must divine it.

PEER.

But how oft are divinings beside the mark,—
Then one's carried " ad undas " [1] in middle career.

THE BUTTON-MOULDER.

That is certain, Peer Gynt; in default of divining
The cloven-hoofed gentleman finds his best hook.

PEER.

This matter's excessively complicated.—
See here! I no longer plead being myself;—
It might not be easy to get it proven.
That part of my case I must look on as lost.
But just now, as I wandered alone o'er the heath,
I felt my conscience-shoe pinching me;
I said to myself: After all, you're a sinner——

THE BUTTON-MOULDER.

You seem bent on beginning all over again——

PEER.

No, very far from it; a great one I mean;
Not only in deeds, but in words and desires.
I've lived a most damnable life abroad——

THE BUTTON-MOULDER.

Perhaps; I must ask you to show me the
schedule !

[1] So in original.

PEER.

Well well, give me time; I will find out a parson,
Confess with all speed, and then bring you his
    voucher.

THE BUTTON-MOULDER.

Ay, if you can bring me that, then it is clear
You may yet escape from the casting-ladle.
But Peer, I'd my orders——

PEER.

          The paper is old ;
It dates no doubt from a long past period ;—
At one time I lived with disgusting slackness,
Went playing the prophet, and trusted in Fate.
Well, may I try?

THE BUTTON-MOULDER.

          But—— !

PEER.

          My dear, good man,
I'm sure you can't have so much to do.
Here, in this district, the air is so bracing,
It adds an ell to the people's ages.
Recollect what the Justedal parson wrote :
"It's seldom that any one dies in this valley."

THE BUTTON-MOULDER.

To the next cross-roads then ; but not a step
    further.

PEER.

A priest I must catch, if it be with the tongs.
                [*He starts running.*

SCENE TENTH.

A heather-clad hillside with a path following the
windings of the ridge.

PEER.

This may come in useful in many ways,
Said Esben as he picked up a magpie's wing.
Who could have thought one's account of sins
Would come to one's aid on the last night of all?
Well, whether or no, it's a ticklish business;
A move from the frying-pan [1] into the fire;—
But then there's a proverb of well-tried validity
Which says that as long as there's life there is
     hope.

A LEAN PERSON *in a priest's cassock, kilted-*
     up high, and with a birding-net over his
     shoulder, comes hurrying along the ridge.

PEER.

Who goes there?   A priest with a fowling-net!
Hei, hop!   I'm the spoilt child of fortune indeed!
Good evening, Herr Pastor! the path is bad——

THE LEAN ONE.

Ah yes; but what wouldn't one do for a soul?

PEER.

Aha! then there's some one bound heavenwards?

THE LEAN ONE.

                                        No;
I hope he is taking a different road.

Literally, "the ashes."

PEER.

May I walk with Herr Pastor a bit of the way?

THE LEAN ONE.

With pleasure; I'm partial to company.

PEER.

I should like to consult you——

THE LEAN ONE.

Heraus![1]   Go ahead!

PEER.

You see here before you a good sort of man.
The laws of the state I have strictly observed,
Have made no acquaintance with fetters or
    bolts;——
But it happens at times that one misses one's
    footing
And stumbles——

THE LEAN ONE.

Ah yes; that occurs to the best of us.

PEER.

Now these trifles you see——

THE LEAN ONE.

Only trifles?

PEER.

Yes;

From sinning *en gros*[1] I have ever refrained.

THE LEAN ONE.

Oh then, my dear fellow, pray leave me in
    peace;——

So in original.

I'm not the person you seem to think me.—
You look at my fingers? What see you in them?

PEER.

A nail-system somewhat extremely developed.

THE LEAN ONE.

And now? You are casting a glance at my feet?

PEER.
[*Pointing.*]

That's a natural hoof?

THE LEAN ONE.

So I flatter myself.

PEER.
[*Raises his hat.*]

I'd have taken my oath you were simply a parson;
And I find I've the honour——. Well, best is
    best ;—
When the hall door stands wide,—shun the
    kitchen way;
When the king's to be met with,—avoid the
    lackey.

THE LEAN ONE.

Your hand ! You appear to be free from prejudice.
Say on then, my friend; in what way can I serve
    you?
Now you mustn't ask me for wealth or power;
I couldn't supply them although I should hang
    for it.
You can't think how slack the whole business is ;—
Transactions have dwindled most pitiably.
Nothing doing in souls; only now and again
A stray one——

PEER.

The race has improved so remarkably ?

THE LEAN ONE.

No, just the reverse; it's sunk shamefully low ;—
The majority end in a casting-ladle.

PEER.

Ah yes—I have heard that ladle mentioned ;
In fact, 'twas the cause of my coming to you.

THE LEAN ONE.

Speak out !

PEER.

If it were not too much to ask,
I should like——

THE LEAN ONE.

A harbour of refuge ? eh ?

PEER.

You've guessed my petition before I have asked.
You tell me the business is going awry ;
So I daresay you will not be over-particular.

THE LEAN ONE.

But, my dear——

PEER.

My demands are in no way excessive.
I shouldn't insist on a salary ;
But treatment as friendly as things will permit.

THE LEAN ONE.

A fire in your room ?

PEER.

       Not too much fire ;—and chiefly
The power of departing in safety and peace,—
The right, as the phrase goes, of freely with-
    drawing
Should an opening offer for happier days.

THE LEAN ONE.

My dear friend, I vow I'm sincerely distressed ;
But you cannot imagine how many petitions
Of similar purport good people send in,
When they're quitting the scene of their earthly
    activity.

PEER.

But now that I think of my past career,
I feel I've an absolute claim to admission——

THE LEAN ONE.

'Twas but trifles, you said——

PEER.

          In a certain sense ;—
But, now I remember, I've trafficked in slaves——

THE LEAN ONE.

There are men that have trafficked in wills and
    souls,
But who bungled it so that they failed to get in.

PEER.

I've shipped Bramah-figures in plenty to China.

THE LEAN ONE.

Mere wish-wash again ! Why, we laugh at such
    things.

There are people that ship off far gruesomer
    figures
In sermons, in art, and in literature,
Yet have to stay out in the cold——

PEER.

Ah, but then,
Do you know—I once went and set up as a
    prophet !

THE LEAN ONE.

In foreign parts ?   Humbug !   Why most people's
    Sehen
Ins Blaue [1] ends in the casting-ladle.
If you've no more than that to rely upon,
With the best of good will, I can't possibly house you.

PEER.

But hear this : In a shipwreck—I clung to a
    boat's keel,—
And it's written: A drowning man grasps at a
    straw,—
Furthermore it is written : You're nearest your-
    self,—
So I half-way divested a cook of his life.

THE LEAN ONE.

It were all one to me if a kitchen-maid
You had half-way divested of something else.
What sort of stuff is this half-way jargon,
Saving your presence ?   Who, think you, would
    care
To throw away dearly-bought fuel, in times
Like these, on such spiritless rubbish as this ?
There now, don't be enraged ; 'twas your sins that
        I scoffed at ;

So in original.

And excuse my speaking my mind so bluntly.—
Come, my dearest friend, banish this stuff from
    your head,[1]
And get used to the thought of the casting-ladle.
What would you gain if I lodged you and boarded
    you ?
Consider; I know you're a sensible man.
Well, you'd keep your memory; that's so far
    true ;—
But the retrospect o'er recollection's domain
Would be, both for heart and for intellect,
What the Swedes call " Mighty poor sport "[2]
    indeed.
You have nothing either to howl or to smile about ;
No cause for rejoicing nor yet for despair ;
Nothing to make you feel hot or cold ;
Only a sort of a something to fret over.

Peer.

It is written : It's never so easy to know
Where the shoe is tight that one isn't wearing.

The Lean One.

Very true ; I have—praise be to so-and-so !—
No occasion for more than a single odd shoe.
But it's lucky we happened to speak of shoes ;
It reminds me that I must be hurrying on ;—
I'm after a roast that I hope will prove fat ;
So I really mustn't stand gossiping here.—

Peer,

And may one inquire, then, what sort of sin-diet
The man has been fattened on ?

Literally, "knock out that tooth."
" Bra litet rolig."

THE LEAN ONE.

                              I understand
He has been himself both by night and by day,
And that, after all, is the principal point.

PEER.

Himself? Then do such folks belong to your
    parish ?

THE LEAN ONE.

That depends; the door, at least, stands ajar for
    them.
Remember, in two ways a man can be
Himself—there's a right and wrong side to the
    jacket.
You know they have lately discovered in Paris
A way to take portraits by help of the sun.
One can either produce a straightforward picture,
Or else what is known as a negative one.
In the latter the lights and the shades are re-
    versed,
And they're apt to seem ugly to commonplace
    eyes ;
But for all that the likeness is latent in them,
And all you require is to bring it out.
If, then, a soul shall have pictured itself
In the course of its life by the negative method,
The plate is not therefore entirely cashiered,—
But without more ado they consign it to me.
For ulterior treatment I take it in hand,
And by suitable methods effect its development.
I steam it, I dip it, I burn it, I scour it,
With sulphur and other ingredients like that,
Till the image appears which the plate was de-
    signed for,—
That, namely, which people call positive.

But for one who, like you, has smudged himself out,
Neither sulphur nor potash avails in the least.

PEER.

I see ; one must come to you black as a raven
To turn out a white ptarmigan ?   Pray what's the
      name
Inscribed 'neath the negative counterfeit
That you're now to transfer to the positive side?

THE LEAN ONE.

The name's Peter [1] Gynt.

PEER.

            Peter Gynt ?   Indeed ?
Is Herr Gynt himself ?

THE LEAN ONE.

            Yes, he vows he is.

PEER.

Well, he's one to be trusted, that same Herr
      Peter.

THE LEAN ONE.

You know him, perhaps?

PEER.

            Oh yes, after a fashion ;—
One knows all sorts of people.

THE LEAN ONE.

            I'm pressed for time ;
Where saw you him last ?

_____
[1] So in original.

PEER.

It was down at the Cape.

THE LEAN ONE.

Di Buona Speranza?

PEER.

Just so; but he sails
Very shortly again, if I'm not mistaken

THE LEAN ONE.

I must hurry off then without delay.
I only hope I may catch him in time!
That Cape of Good Hope—I could never abide it;—
It's ruined by missionaries from Stavanger.

[*He rushes off southwards.*

PEER.

The stupid hound! There he takes to his heels
With his tongue lolling out. He'll be finely sold.
It delights me to humbug an ass like that.
He to give himself airs, and to lord it forsooth!
He's a mighty lot, truly, to swagger about!
He'll scarcely grow fat at his present trade ;—
He'll soon drop from his perch with his whole
     apparatus.—
H'm, I'm not over-safe in the saddle either;
I'm expelled, one may say, from self-owning
     nobility.[1]

[*A shooting star is seen ; he nods after it.*
Greet all friends from Peer Gynt, Brother Starry-
     Flash!

---

[1] "*Selv*ejer-Adlen." "Selvejer" (literally, "self-owner") means
a freeholder, as opposed to a "husmand" or tenant. There is
of course a play upon words in the original.

To flash forth, to go out, and be naught at a gulp—
> [*Pulls himself together as though in terror,
> and goes deeper in among the mists; still-
> ness for awhile; then he cries:*

Is there no one, no one in all the whirl,—
In the void no one, and no one in heaven—!
> [*He comes forward again further down,
> throws his hat upon the ground, and tears
> at his hair. By degrees a stillness comes
> over him.*

So unspeakably poor, then, a soul can go
Back to nothingness, into the grey of the mist.
Thou beautiful earth, be not angry with me
That I trampled thy grasses to no avail.
Thou beautiful sun, thou hast squandered away
Thy glory of light in an empty hut.
There was no one within it to hearten and warm;—
The owner, they tell me, was never at home.
Beautiful sun and beautiful earth,
You were foolish to bear and give light to my
    mother.
The spirit is niggard and nature lavish;
And dearly one pays for one's birth with one's life.—
I will clamber up high, to the dizziest peak;
I will look once more on the rising sun,
Gaze till I'm tired o'er the promised land;
Then try to get snowdrifts piled up over me.
They can write above them : " Here No One lies
    buried ";
And afterwards,—then——! Let things go as
    they can.

CHURCH-GOERS.

[*Singing on the forest path.*]
Oh, morning thrice blest,
When the tongues of God's kingdom

Struck the earth like to flaming steel!
From the earth to his dwelling
Now the heirs' song ascendeth
In the tongue of the kingdom of God.

PEER.
[*Crouches as in terror.*]
Never look there! there all's desert and waste.—
I fear I was dead long before I died.
        [*Tries to slink in among the bushes, but
        comes upon the cross-roads.*

THE BUTTON-MOULDER.
Good morning, Peer Gynt! Where's the list of
    your sins?
PEER.
Do you think that I haven't been whistling and
    shouting
As hard as I could?

THE BUTTON-MOULDER.
                And met no one at all?

PEER.
Not a soul but a tramping photographer.

THE BUTTON-MOULDER.
Well, the respite is over.

PEER.
                Ay, everything's over.
The owl smells the daylight. Just list to the
    hooting!
THE BUTTON-MOULDER.
It's the matin-bell ringing——

PEER.

[*Pointing.*]
    What's that shining yonder?

THE BUTTON-MOULDER.

Only light from a hut.

PEER.

    And that wailing sound——?

THE BUTTON-MOULDER.

But a woman singing.

PEER.

        Ay, there—there I'll find
The list of my sins——

THE BUTTON-MOULDER.

[*Seizing him.*]
        Set your house in order!
[*They have come out of the underwood, and
   are standing near the hut. Day is
   dawning.*

PEER.

Set my house in order? It's there! Away.
Get you gone! Though your ladle were huge as a
    coffin,
It were too small, I tell you, for me and my sins.

THE BUTTON-MOULDER.

Well, to the third cross-road, Peer; but then——.
           [*Turns aside and goes.*

PEER.

[*Approaches the hut.*]
Forward and back, and it's just as far.

Out and in, and it's just as strait.   [*Stops*
No!—like a wild, an unending lament,
Is the thought : to come back, to go in, to go home.
          [*Takes a few steps on, but stops again.*
Round about, said the Boyg!
                    [*Hears singing in the hut.*
                    Ah no ; this time at least
Right through, though the path may be never so
     strait !
          [*He runs towards the hut ; at the same
          moment* Solveig *appears in the doorway,
          dressed for church, with a psalm-book
          wrapped in a kerchief, and a staff in her
          hand.   She stands there erect and mild.*

PEER.

[*Flings himself down on the threshold.*]
Hast thou doom for a sinner, then speak it forth !

SOLVEIG.

He is here ! He is here ! Oh, to God be the
     praise !
          [*Stretches out her arms as though groping
          for him.*

PEER.

Cry out all my sins and my trespasses !

SOLVEIG.

In nought hast thou sinned, oh my own only boy.
          [*Gropes for him again, and finds him.*

THE BUTTON-MOULDER.

[*Behind the house.*]
The sin-list, Peer Gynt ?

PEER.

Cry aloud my crime !

SOLVEIG.

[*Sits down beside him.*]

Thou hast made all my life as a beautiful song.
Blessëd be thou that at last thou hast come !
Blessëd, thrice blessëd our Whitsun-morn meeting!

PEER.

Then I am lost !

SOLVEIG.

There is one that rules all things.

PEER.

[*Laughs.*]

Lost !   Unless thou canst answer riddles.

SOLVEIG.

Tell me them.

PEER.

Tell them !   Come on !   To be sure '
Canst thou tell where Peer Gynt has been since
we parted ?

SOLVEIG.

Been ?

PEER.

With his destiny's seal on his brow ;
Been, as in God's thought he first sprang forth !
Canst thou tell me? If not, I must get me home,—
Go down to the mist-shrouded regions.

SOLVEIG.

[*Smiling.*]

Oh, that riddle is easy.

PEER.

Then tell what thou knowest!
Where was I, as myself, as the whole man, the true
man?
Where was I, with God's sigil upon my brow?

SOLVEIG.

In my faith, in my hope, and in my love.[1]

PEER.

[*Starts back.*]
What sayest thou——? Peace! These are jug-
gling words.
Thou art mother thyself to the man that's there.

SOLVEIG.

Ay, that I am; but who is his father?
Surely he that forgives at the mother's prayer.

PEER.

[*A light shines in his face; he cries:*]
My mother; my wife; oh, thou innocent woman!—
In thy love—oh, there hide me, hide me!
        [*Clings to her and hides his face in her lap.
        A long silence.   The sun rises.*

SOLVEIG.

[*Sings softly.*]
Sleep thou, dearest boy of mine!
I will cradle thee, I will watch thee——

"I min Tro, i mit Håb og i min Kjærlighed."
    We have entirely sacrificed the metre of the line, feeling it
impossible to mar its simplicity by any padding. "Kjærlighed"
also means "charity," in the biblical sense.

The boy has been sitting on his mother's lap.
They two have been playing all the life-day long.

The boy has been resting at his mother's breast
All the life-day long.   God's blessing on my joy

The boy has been lying close in to my heart,
All the life-day long.   He is weary now.

Sleep thou, dearest boy of mine !
I will cradle thee, I will watch thee.

THE BUTTON-MOULDER'S VOICE.
[*Behind the house.*]
At the last cross-road we will meet again, Peer;
And then we'll see whether——; I say no more.

SOLVEIG.
[*Sings louder in the full daylight.*]
I will cradle thee, I will watch thee;
Sleep and dream thou, dear my boy !

THE END.

APPENDIX.

[THE stories of Peer Gynt and Gudbrand Glesnë both occur in Asbjörnsen's "Reindeer-hunting in the Rondë Hills" (*Norske Huldre-Eventyr og Folkesagn,* Christiania, 1848). They are told by the peasant guides or gillies who accompany a shooting-party into the mountains—the first by Peer Fugleskjelle, the second by Thor Ulvsvolden. Our translation of Asbjörnsen's "Peer Gynt" is based on Mr. H. L. Brækstad's version, published in *Round the Yule Log*, London, 1881.]

PEER GYNT.

IN the old days there lived in Kvam a hunter, whose name was Peer Gynt. He was always up in the mountains shooting bears and elks ; for in those days there were more forests on the mountains to harbour such wild beasts. One time, late in the autumn, long after the cattle had been driven home, Peer set out for the hills. Every one had left the uplands except three sæter-girls. When Peer came up towards Hövring, where he was to pass the night in a sæter, it was so dark that he could not see his fist before him, and the dogs fell to barking and baying so that it was quite uncanny. All of a sudden he ran against something, and when he put his hand out he felt it was cold and slippery and big. Yet he did not seem to have strayed from the road, so he couldn't think what this could be ; but unpleasant it was at any rate.

" Who is it ?" asked Peer, for he felt it moving.

" Oh, it's the Boyg," [1] was the answer.

Peer was no wiser for this, but skirted along it for a bit, thinking that somewhere he must be able to pass. Suddenly he ran against something again, and when he put out his hand, it too was big, and cold, and slippery.

" Who is it ?" asked Peer Gynt.

" Oh, it's the Boyg," was the answer again.

" Well, straight or crooked, you'll have to let me pass," said Peer ; for he understood that he was walking in a ring, and that the Boyg had curled itself round the sæter. Thereupon it shifted a little, so that Peer got past. When he came inside the sæter it was no lighter there than outside. He was feeling along the wall for a place to hang up his gun and his bag ; but as he was groping his way forward he again felt something cold, and big, and slippery.

" Who is it ? " shouted Peer.

" Oh, it's the great Boyg," was the answer. Where-ever he put his hands out er tried to get past, he felt the Boyg encircling him.

" It's not very pleasant to be here," thought Peer, "since this Boyg is both out and in ; but I think I can make short work of the nuisance."

So he took his gun and went out again, groping his way till he found the creature's head.

" What are you ? " asked Peer.

" Oh, I am the big Boyg from Etnedale," said the Troll-Monster. Peer did not lose a moment, but fired three shots right into its head.

[1] See footnote, p. xxvi.

"Fire another," said the Boyg. But Peer knew better ; if he had fired another shot, the bullet would have rebounded against himself.

Thereupon Peer and his dogs took hold of the Troll-Monster and dragged him out, so that they could get into the sæter. Meanwhile there was jeering and laughing in all the hills around.

"Peer Gynt dragged hard, but the dogs dragged harder," said a voice.

Next morning he went out stalking. When he came out on the uplands he saw a girl, who was calling some sheep up a hillside. But when he came to the place the girl was gone and the sheep too, and he saw nothing but a great flock of bears.

"Well, I never saw bears in a flock before," thought Peer to himself. When he came nearer, they had all disappeared except one.

> "Look after your pig :
> Peer Gynt is out
> with his gun so big,"[1]

shouted a voice over in a hillock.

"Oh, it'll be a bad business for Peer, but not for my pig ; for he hasn't washed himself to-day," said another voice in the hill. Peer washed his hands with the water he had, and shot the bear. There was more laughter and jeering in the hill.

"You should have looked after your pig !" cried a voice.

"I didn't remember he had a water-jug between his legs," answered the other.

Peer skinned the bear and buried the carcass among the stones, but the head and the hide he took with him. On his way home he met a fox.

---

[1] Literally, "with his tail." A gun loosely slung over the shoulder bears a certain resemblance to a tail sticking up in the air.

" Look at my lamb, how fat it is," said a voice in a hill.

" Look at that gun[1] of Peer's, how high it is," said a voice in another hill, just as Peer took aim and shot the fox. He skinned the fox and took the skin with him, and when he came to the sæter he put the heads on the wall outside, with their jaws gaping. Then he lighted a fire and put a pot on to boil some soup, but the chimney smoked so terribly that he could scarcely keep his eyes open, and so he had to set wide a small window. Suddenly a Troll came and poked his nose in through the window ; it was so long that it reached across the room to the fireplace.

"Here's a proper snout for you to see," said the Troll.

" And here's proper soup for you to taste," said Peer Gynt ; and he poured the whole potful of soup over the Troll's nose. The Troll ran away howling ; but in all the hills around there was jeering and laughing and voices shouting—

" Soup-snout Gyri ! Soup-snout Gyri ! "

All was quiet now for a while ; but before long there was a great noise and hubbub outside again. Peer looked out and saw that there was a cart there, drawn by bears. They hoisted up the Troll-Monster, and carted him away into the mountain. Just then a bucket of water came down the chimney and put out the fire, so that Peer was left in the dark. Then a jeering and laughing began in all the corners of the room, and a voice said—

" It'll go no better with Peer now than with the sæter-girls at Vala."

Peer made up the fire again, took his dogs with him, shut up the house, and set off northward to the Vala sæter, where the three girls were. When he had

[1] Literally, " tail."

gone some distance he saw such a glare of light that
it seemed to him the sæter must be on fire. Just
then he came across a pack of wolves ; some of them
he shot, and some he knocked on the head. When he
came to the Vala sæter he found it pitch dark ; there
was no sign of any fire ; but there were four strangers
in the house carrying on with the sæter-girls. They
were four Hill-Trolls, and their names were Gust of
Værë, Tron of the Valfjeld, Tjöstöl Aabakken, and
Rolf Eldförpungen. Gust of Værë was standing at
the door to keep watch, while the others were in with
the girls courting. Peer fired at Gust, but missed
him, and Gust ran away. When Peer came inside he
found the Trolls carrying on desperately with the
girls. Two of the girls were terribly frightened and
were saying their prayers, but the third, who was
called Mad Kari, wasn't afraid ; she said they might
come there for all she cared ; she would like to see
what stuff there was in such fellows. But when the
Trolls found that Peer was in the room they began to
howl, and told Eldförpungen to make up the fire.
At that instant the dogs set upon Tjöstöl and pulled
him over on his back into the fireplace, so that the
ashes and sparks flew up all round him.

"Did you see my snakes, Peer ? " asked Tron of
the Valfjeld—that was what he called the wolves.

"You shall go the same way as your snakes," said
Peer, and shot him ; and then he killed Aabakken
with the butt-end of his rifle. Eldförpungen had
escaped up the chimney. After this Peer took the
girls back to their homes, for they didn't dare to stay
any longer up at the sæter.

Shortly before Christmas-time Peer set out again.
He had heard of a farm on the Dovrefjeld which was
invaded by such a number of Trolls every Christmas-

eve that the people of the farm had to turn out and get shelter with some of their neighbours. He was anxious to go there, for he was very keen upon the Trolls. He dressed himself in some old ragged clothes, and took with him a tame white bear that he had, as well as an awl, some pitch, and waxed twine. When he came to the farm he went in and begged for houseroom.

" God help us ! " said the farmer ; " we can't put you up. We have to clear out of the house ourselves, for every blessëd Christmas-eve the whole place is full of Trolls."

But Peer Gynt said he thought he should be able to clear the house of Trolls ; and then he got leave to stay, and they gave him a pig's skin into the bargain. The bear lay down behind the fireplace, and Peer took out his awl, and pitch, and twine, and set to making a big shoe, that took the whole pig's skin. He put a strong rope in for laces, so that he could pull the shoe tight together at the top ; and he had a couple of handspikes ready.

All of a sudden the Trolls came, with a fiddle and a fiddler ; some began dancing, while others fell to eating the Christmas fare on the table ; some fried bacon, and some fried frogs and toads, and other disgusting things : these were the Christmas dainties they had brought with them. In the meantime some of the Trolls found the shoe Peer had made ; they thought it must be for a very big foot. Then they all wanted to try it on ; and when each of them had put a foot into it, Peer tightened the rope, shoved one of the handspikes into it, and twisted it up till they were all stuck fast in the shoe.

Just then the bear put his nose out and smelt the fry.

" Will you have a sausage, white pussy ? " said one of the Trolls, and threw a red-hot frog right into the bear's jaws.

" Claw and smite, Bruin ! " said Peer Gynt.

And then the bear got into such a rage that he rushed at the Trolls and smote and clawed them all, and Peer Gynt took the other handspike and hammered away at them as if he wanted to beat their brains out. So the Trolls had to clear out, and Peer stayed and enjoyed himself on the Christmas cheer the whole feast-time. After that the Trolls were not heard of again for many years. The farmer had a light-coloured mare, and Peer advised him to breed from her, and let her foals in their turn run and breed among the hills there.

Many years afterwards, about Christmas-time, the farmer was out in the forest cutting wood for the feast-time, when a Troll came towards him and shouted—

" Have you got that big white pussy of yours yet ? "

" Yes, she's at home behind the stove," said the farmer ; "and she's got seven kittens now, much bigger and fiercer than herself."

" We'll never come to you any more, then," shouted the Troll.

" That Peer Gynt was a strange one," said Anders. " He was such an out-and-out tale-maker and yarn-spinner, you couldn't have helped laughing at him. He always made out that he himself had been mixed up in all the stories that people said had happened in the olden times."

GUDBRAND GLESNË.

"THERE was a hunter in the West-Hills," said Thor Ulvsvolden, " called Gudbrand Glesnë. He was married to the grandmother of the lad you saw at the sæter yesterday evening, and a first-rate hunter they say he was. One autumn he came across a huge buck. He shot at it, and from the way it fell he couldn't tell but that it was stone dead. So he went up to it, and, as one often does, seated himself astride on its back, and was just drawing his knife to cleave the neck-bone from the skull. But no sooner had he sat down than up it jumped, threw its horns back, and jammed him down between them, so that he was fixed as in an arm-chair. Then it rushed away ; for the bullet had only grazed the beast's head, so that it had fallen in a swoon. Never any man had such a ride[1] as that Gudbrand had. Away they went in the teeth of the wind, over the ugliest glaciers and moraines. Then the beast dashed along the Gjende-edge ; and now Gudbrand prayed to the Lord, for he thought he would never see sun or moon again. But at last the reindeer took to the water and swam straight across with the hunter on its back. By this time he had got his knife drawn, and the moment the buck set foot on shore, he plunged it into its neck, and it dropped dead. But you may be sure Gudbrand Glesnë wouldn't have taken that ride again, not for all the riches in the world.

"I have heard a story like that in England, about a deer-stalker that became a deer-rider," said Sir Tottenbroom.[2]

[1] " Skyds "—conveyance.
[2] An English sportsman who accompanied Asbjörnsen on his rambles.

"Bliecher, in Jutland, tells a similar one," I said.

"But what sort of a place was this Gjender-edge you spoke of, Thor ? " he interrupted me.

"Gjende-edge, you mean ? " asked Thor.   "It's the ridge [1] of a mountain lying between the Gjende-lakes, and so horribly narrow and steep that if you stand on it and drop a stone from each hand, they will roll down into the lakes, one on each side.   The reindeer-hunters go over it in fine weather, otherwise it's impassable ; but there was a devil of a fellow up in Skiager—Ole Storebråten was his name—who went over it carrying a full-sized reindeer on his shoulders."

"How high is it above the lakes ? " asked Sir Tottenbroom.

"Oh, it's not nearly so high as the Rondë-hills," said Thor.   "But it's over seven hundred ells high."

---

[1] " Rygge "—backbone, *arête.*